ARABIAN SOCIETY

IN THE MIDDLE AGES

جَمَالُ ٱلرَّجُلِ فَصَاحَةُ لِسَانِهِ

ARABIAN SOCIETY

IN THE MIDDLE AGES

STUDIES FROM

THE THOUSAND AND ONE NIGHTS

BY

EDWARD WILLIAM LANE

EDITED BY

STANLEY LANE-POOLE

INTRODUCTION BY

C. E. BOSWORTH

CURZON PRESS : LONDON
HUMANITIES PRESS : NEW JERSEY

Paperback edition
First published 1987 in the United Kingdom by
Curzon Press Ltd, 42 Gray's Inn Road, London WC1

ISBN 0 7007 0195 8

First published 1987 in the United States of America by
Humanities Press International Inc, 171 First Avenue
Atlantic Highlands, NJ 07716

ISBN 0 391 03462 6

Library of Congress Cataloging in Publication Data

Lane, Edward William, 1801–1876.
Arabian society in the Middle Ages.

Reprint. Originally published: 1883. With new introd.
by C. E. Bosworth.
Bibliography: p.
Includes index.
1. Islamic Empire—Social life and customs.
2. Egypt—Social life and customs. 3. Arabian
nights. I. Lane-Poole, Stanley, 1854–1931.
II. Title.
DS36.855.L36 1986 939'.4 86-21103
ISBN 0-391-03462-6 (pbk.)

Printed and bound in Great Britain by
Biddles Ltd, Guildford and King's Lynn

INTRODUCTION

As Stanley Lane-Poole explains in his Preface, his task in compiling the present book a few years after its author's death aimed at making available, in a concise form, the immense erudition which his great-uncle Edward William Lane had put into the explanatory *Notes* for his translation of *The Thousand and One Nights*. Lane had utilized as the main basis for this the Arabic text printed at the press of Būlāq in the suburbs of Cairo established by the Pasha Muḥammad 'Alī, but had enriched it by a copious commentary. Since the stories making up the *Nights* illustrate almost the whole gamut of public and settled domestic life in the Arab Middle Ages, from the opulent surroundings of Caliphs and Sultans to the humblest dwellings of petty tradesmen and bazaar artisans, Lane was able to construct on these foundations a remarkably detailed picture of society as it functioned in the urban centres of Mediaeval Islam. (The life of the nomadic Bedouins and rural cultivators in the villages, who numerically must have constituted the bulk of the population in the Arab lands, is by contrast hardly touched upon, and in this respect, Lane's picture of Islamic society—both in these *Notes* and in his great work based on his years of residence in Cairo, 1825–8 and 1833–5, as

"Manṣūr Efendi", his *Manners and Customs of the Modern Egyptians*—is a partial one only.) Contemporary critics and reviewers, as Leila Ahmed has recently observed (*Edward W. Lane: A Study of his Life and Work and British Ideas of the Middle East in the Nineteenth Century*, London, New York and Beirut 1978, 141 ff.), tended to regard the *Notes* as more important than the translated text of the *Nights*, which had of course been well known in the West for over a century since Antoine Galland's French version. Lane naturally utilized for his *Notes* his personal experiences of life in a Cairo which was in its last phase of pre-modern society before the westernizing policies of Muḥammad 'Alī and his family and the opening-up of Egypt to foreign persons, capital and ideas began to erode and transmute the fabric of life, at least in such great urban centres as Cairo and Alexandria. He also drew upon his profound knowledge of classical Arabic literature and the cultural milieu from which it sprang, explored through his interest in philology and as a basis for his *magnum opus*, the regrettably unfinished *Arabic-English Lexicon*; an intellectual tradition which extended almost to his own time in Egypt in the personage of a traditional-type historian like 'Abd al-Raḥmān al-Jabartī (d. 1825 or 1826), whose chronicle of military and political events in late Mamlūk Egypt Lane knew and cited.

The value of the present book lies both in its conciseness and in the remarkable degree of detachedness from his own firmly-held Christian beliefs, even of sympathy for many aspects of a very alien creed and society, which Lane was able to achieve. It displays the great breadth of Lane's reading in the secondary literature of Islamic scholarship in his time—though this was still fairly exiguous in extent compared with the efflorescence of Western orientalist scholarship in the second half of the nineteenth century—and also in the literature of the accounts and journals left by sympathetic European residents and travellers in the Arab Orient, such as the *Letters* of Lady Wortley Montague, the travel accounts of the Swiss orientalist John Lewis Burckhardt and the penetrating accounts of his official service and his travels in the Levant and the Ottoman Balkans by Lane's contemporary, the Scottish diplomat, Member of Parliament, Turkophile and Russophobe David Urquhart.

Lane's book can thus still be commended to readers of a century and a quarter after its author's death as a lucid and, for its time, remarkably dispassionate account of mediaeval Islamic urban society.

C. E. BOSWORTH University of Manchester
1986

PREFACE.

When Mr. Lane translated the "Thousand and One Nights," he was not content with producing a mere rendering of the Arabic text: he saw that the manners and ideas there described required a commentary if they were to become intelligible to an unlearned reader. At the end of each chapter of his translation, therefore, he appended a series of explanatory notes, which often reached the proportions of elaborate essays on the main characteristics of Mohammadan life.

These notes have long been recognized by Orientalists as the most complete picture in existence of Arabian society—or rather of those Arab, Persian, or Greek, but still Mohammadan, conditions of life and boundaries of the mental horizon which are generally distinguished by the name of Arabian. Their position and arrangement, however, scattered as they were through three large volumes, and inserted in the order required not by their subjects but by the tales they illustrated, rendered them difficult to consult, and cumbrous, if not impossible, to read consecutively. It has often been suggested that a reprint of the principal notes, in a convenient form and in natural sequence, would be a welcome addition to the scholar's as well as to the general library. The publication of a new impression of the "Thousand and One Nights" presented an opportunity for discussing the project; and the result is the present volume.

My task, as editor, has been a simple one. I have rejected only those notes which have no value apart from the main work—glossarial notes, for instance, giving the English of the proper names occurring in the Arabian Nights; disquisitions on the probable date of the composition of the tales; and others inseparably connected with the stories themselves. The rest I have arranged in a series of chapters, interweaving the shorter notes in the longer, and giving as far as possible an air of unity to each division. Beyond such verbal alterations as were required by the separation of the notes from the text to which they referred, occasional changes in punctuation, and a slight alteration in the spelling of Oriental names in accordance with my great-uncle's latest method, I have not interfered with the form of the notes as they appeared in the edition of 1859. Such insignificant changes as I have made, I think I may state with confidence, would have been approved by the author. Beyond a few notes distinguished by square brackets, a new and very minute index (in which all Arabic words are explained), and a list of the authorities quoted, I have added nothing of my own.

It may be objected to the title of the book that a considerable part of the notes is composed of recollections of Mr. Lane's personal experiences in Cairo in the early part of the present century. The subject-matter, however, is really mediæval. The notes have all the same purpose: to explain the conditions of life and society as they were at the time when the "Thousand and One Nights" assumed their present collected form. Upon various grounds Mr. Lane placed this redaction or composition at about the end of the fifteenth century. Accordingly a large proportion of these notes consist of extracts from the more famous Arabic historians and other authors of the later Middle Ages, such as Ibn El-Jowzee (who died in A.D. 1256), El-Ḳazweenee (1283), Ibn-el-Wardee (1348), Ibn-Khaldoon (1406), El-Maḳreezee (1441), Es-Suyooṭee (1505), who all knew Arabian society in precisely the state described in the "Thousand and One Nights." Most of these authorities were unpublished when the notes were written, and Mr. Lane's quotations are from manuscripts in his own possession. Some are still inedited; and though many have been printed at the Booláḳ Press and elsewhere, it is surprising how little they have been used by European authors.

To the records of these mediæval writers, Mr. Lane added the results of his personal experience; and in doing so he was guilty of no anachronism: for the Arabian Society in which a Saladin, a Beybars, a Barḳooḳ, and a Ḳait-Bey moved, and of which the native historians have preserved so full and graphic a record, survived almost unchanged to the time of Moḥammad 'Alee, when Mr. Lane spent many years of intimate acquaintance among the people of Cairo. The life that he saw was the same as that described by El-Maḳreezee and Es-Suyooṭee; and the purely Muslim society in which Mr. Lane preferred to move was in spirit, in custom, and in all essentials the same society that once hailed a Hároon er-Rasheed, a Jaạfar el-Barmekee, and an Aboo-Nuwás, among its members. The continuity of Arabian social tradition was practically unbroken from almost the beginning of the Khalifate to the present century, at least in such a metropolis of Islám as Cairo, or as Damascus or Baghdad. European influence has been busy in demolishing it. Cairo has long been trying to become a bastard Paris instead of the picturesque city of El-Mo'izz and Ṣaláḥ-ed-Deen, and to forget its traditions of the palmy days of Islám and its memorials of the chivalrous heroes of crusading times. It would be impossible now to gather the minute details of a purely Mohammadan society which Mr. Lane found ready to his eye and hand; and it is therefore the more fortunate that the record of Arabian Society, as it was during the Khalifate and under the rule of the Memlooks in the Middle Ages, and as it continued to be in Egypt to the days of Moḥammad 'Alee, was faithfully preserved in the "Manners and Customs of the Modern Egyptians," and in the notes to the "Thousand and One Nights," which are here for the first time presented in a separate and consecutive form.

STANLEY LANE-POOLE.

CONTENTS.

CHAPTER I.

RELIGION.

CHAPTER II.

DEMONOLOGY.

CHAPTER III.

SAINTS.

CHAPTER IV.

MAGIC.

CHAPTER V.

COSMOGRAPHY.

CHAPTER VI.

LITERATURE.

CHAPTER VII.

FEASTING AND MERRYMAKING.

CHAPTER XI.

CEREMONIES OF DEATH.

ARABIAN SOCIETY IN THE MIDDLE AGES.

CHAPTER I.

RELIGION.

The confession of the Muslim's faith is briefly made in these words,—"There is no deity but God: Moḥammad is God's Apostle,"—which imply a belief and observance of everything that Moḥammad taught to be the word or will of God. In the opinion of those who are commonly called orthodox, and termed Sunnees, the Mohammadan code is founded upon the Ḳur-án, the Traditions of the Prophet, the concordance of his principal early disciples, and the decisions which have been framed from analogy or comparison. The Sunnees consist of four sects, Ḥanafees, Sháfi'ees, Málikees, and Hambelees, so called after the names of their respective founders. The other sects, who are called Shiya'ees (an appellation particularly given to the Persian sect, but also used to designate generally all who are not Sunnees), are regarded nearly in the same light as those who do not profess El-Islám (the Mohammadan faith); that is, as destined to eternal punishment.

I. The Mohammadan faith embraces the following points:—

1. Belief in God, who is without beginning or end, the sole Creator and Lord of the universe, having absolute power, and knowledge, and glory, and perfection.

2. Belief in his Angels, who are impeccable beings, created of light; and Genii (Jinn), who are peccable, created of smokeless fire. The Devils, whose chief is Iblees, or Satan, are evil Genii.[1]

3. Belief in his Prophets and Apostles;[2] the most distinguished of whom are Adam, Noah, Abraham, Moses, Jesus, and Moḥammad. Jesus is held to be more excellent than any of those who preceded him, to have been born of a virgin, and to be the Messiah and the word of God and a Spirit proceeding from him, but not partaking of his essence and not to be called the Son of God. Moḥammad is held to be more excellent than all, the last and greatest of prophets and apostles, the most excellent of the creatures of God.

4. Belief in his Scriptures, which are his uncreated

[1] See below, 25 ff.

[2] An Apostle is distinguished from a mere Prophet by his having a *book* revealed to him.

word, revealed to his prophets. Of these there now exist, but held to be greatly corrupted, the Pentateuch of Moses, the Psalms of David, and the Gospels of Jesus Christ; and, in an uncorrupted and incorruptible state, the Ḳur-án, which is held to have abrogated, and to surpass in excellence, all preceding revelations.

5. Belief in the general Resurrection and Judgment, and in future rewards and punishments, chiefly of a corporeal nature: the punishments will be eternal to all but wicked Mohammadans; and none but Mohammadans will enter into a state of happiness.

6. Belief in God's Predestination of all events, both good and evil.

The belief in fate and destiny (el-ḳaḍà wa-l-ḳadar)[1] exercises a most powerful influence upon the actions and character of the Muslims. Many hold that fate is in some respects absolute and unchangeable, in others admitting of alteration; and almost all of them *act* in many of the affairs of life as if this were their belief. In the former case, it is called "el-ḳaḍà el-moḥkam:" in the latter, "el-ḳaḍà el-mubram" (which term, without the expla-

[1] I use two words (perhaps the best that our language affords) to express corresponding Arabic terms, which some persons regard as synonymous, but others distinguish by different shades of meaning. On what I consider the best authority, the word which I render "fate" respects the decrees of God in a general sense; while that which I translate "destiny" relates to the particular applications of those decrees. In such senses these terms are here to be understood when separately employed.

nation here given, might be regarded as exactly synonymous with the former). Hence the Prophet, it is said, prayed to be preserved from the latter, as knowing that it might be changed; and in allusion to this changeable fate, we are told, God says, "God will cancel what He pleaseth, and confirm;"[1] while, on the contrary, the fate which is termed "moḥkam" is appointed "destiny" decreed by God.[2]

Many doctors have argued that destiny respects only the *final state* of a certain portion of men (believers and unbelievers), and that in general man is endowed with free will, which he should exercise according to the laws of God and his own conscience and judgment, praying to God for a blessing on his endeavours, or imploring the intercession of the Prophet or of any of the saints in his favour, and propitiating them by offering alms or sacrifices in their names, relying upon God for the result, which he may then, and then only, attribute to fate or destiny. They hold, therefore, that it is criminal to attempt resistance to the will when its dictates are conformable with the laws of God and our natural consciences and prudence, and so passively to await the fulfilment of God's decrees.—The doctrine of the Ḳur-án and the traditions respecting the decrees of God, or fate and destiny, appears, however, to be that

[1] Ḳur-án, xiii. 39.

[2] El-Insán el-Kámil, by 'Abd-El-Kereem El-Jeelee, quoted by El-Isḥáḳee in his account of Ibráheem Pásha el-Maḳtool.

they are altogether absolute and unchangeable, written in the beginning of the creation on the "Preserved Tablet" in heaven; that God hath predestined every event and action, evil as well as good,—at the same time commanding and approving good, and forbidding and hating evil; and that the "cancelling" mentioned in the preceding paragraph relates (as the context seems to show) to the abrogation of former scriptures or revelations, not of fate. But still it must be held that He hath not predestined the *will;* though He sometimes inclines it to good, and the Devil sometimes inclines it to evil. It is asked, then, If we have the power to will, but not the power to perform otherwise than as God hath predetermined, how can we be regarded as responsible beings? The answer to this is that our actions are judged good or evil according to our intentions, if we have faith: good actions or intentions, it should be added, only increase, and do not cause, our happiness if we are believers; and evil actions or intentions only increase our misery if we are unbelievers or irreligious: for the Muslim holds that he is to be admitted into heaven only by the mercy of God, on account of his faith, and to be rewarded in proportion to his good works.

The Prophet's assertions on the subject of God's decrees are considered of the highest importance as explanatory of the Ḳur-án.—"Whatever is in the universe," said he, "is by the order of God."—"God hath pre-ordained five things on his servants; the duration of life, their actions, their dwelling-places, their travels, and their portions."—"There is not one among you whose sitting-place is not written by God, whether in the fire or in paradise."—Some of the companions of the Prophet, on hearing the last-quoted saying, asked him, "O Prophet, since God hath appointed our places, may we confide in this, and abandon our religious and moral duties?" He answered, "No: because the happy will do good works, and those who are of the miserable will do bad works."

The following of his sayings further illustrate this subject:—"When God hath ordered a creature to die in any particular place, He causeth his wants to direct him to that place."—A companion asked, "O Prophet of God, inform me respecting charms, and the medicines which I swallow, and shields which I make use of for protection, whether they prevent any of the orders of God." Moḥammad answered, "These also are by the order of God." "There is a medicine for every pain: then, when the medicine reaches the pain it is cured by the order of God."[1]—When a Muslim, therefore, feels an inclination to make use of medicine for the cure of a disease, he should do so, in the hope of its being predestined that he shall be so cured.

[1] Mishkát el-Maṣábeeḥ, i. 26–34, 373. [Cp. S. Lane-Poole, "The Speeches and Tabletalk of the Prophet Moḥammad" (1882), 180–182.]

On the predestination of diseases, I find the following curious quotation and remark in a manuscript work [1] by Es-Suyooṭee, who wrote in the fifteenth century, in my possession:—"El-Ḥaleemee says, 'Communicable or contagious diseases are six: small-pox, measles, itch or scab, foul breath or putridity, melancholy, and pestilential maladies; and diseases engendered are also six: leprosy, hectic, epilepsy, gout, elephantiasis, and phthisis.' But this does not contradict the saying of the Prophet, 'There is no transition of diseases by contagion or infection, nor any omen that brings evil:' for the transition here meant is one occasioned by the disease itself; whereas the effect is of God, who causes pestilence to spread when there is intercourse with the diseased."—A Bedawee asked the Prophet, "What is the condition of camels which stay in the deserts? verily you might say they are deer, in health and in cleanness of skin; then they mix with mangy camels, and they become mangy also." Moḥammad said, "What made the first camel mangy?" [2]

Notwithstanding, however, the arguments which have been here adduced, and many others that might be added, declaring or implying the unchangeable nature of all God's decrees, I have found it to be the opinion of my own Muslim friends that God may be induced by supplication to change certain of his

[1] Nuzhet el-Mutaämmil wa-Murshid el-Mutaähhil, section 7.
[2] Mishkát el-Maṣábeeḥ, ii. 381.

decrees, at least those regarding degrees of happiness or misery in this world and the next; and that such is the general opinion appears from a form of prayer which is repeated in the mosques on the eve of the middle (or fifteenth day) of the month of Shaạbán, when it is believed that such portions of God's decrees as constitute the destinies of all living creatures for the ensuing year are confirmed and fixed. In this prayer it is said, "O God, if Thou *hast recorded* me in thy abode, upon 'the Original of the Book' [the Preserved Tablet], miserable or unfortunate or scanted in my sustenance, *cancel,* O God, of thy goodness, my misery and misfortune and scanty allowance of sustenance, and confirm me in thy abode, upon the Original of the Book, as happy and provided for and directed to good,"[1] etc.

The Arabs in general constantly have recourse both to charms and medicines, not only for the cure but also for the prevention of diseases. They have, indeed, a strange passion for medicine, which shows that they do not consider fate as altogether unconditional. Nothing can exceed the earnestness with which they often press a European traveller for a dose; and the more violent the remedy, the better are they pleased. The following case will serve as an example:—Three donkey-drivers, conveying the luggage of two British

[1] For a translation of the whole of this prayer, see my "Account of the Manners and Customs of the Modern Egyptians," ch. xxv.

travellers from Booláḳ to Cairo, opened a bottle which they observed in a basket, and finding it to contain (as they had suspected) brandy, emptied it down their throats: but he who had the last draught, on turning up the bottle, got the tail of a scorpion into his mouth; and, looking through the bottle to his great horror saw that it contained a number of these reptiles, with tarantulas, vipers, and beetles. Thinking that they had poisoned themselves, but not liking to rely upon fate, they persuaded a man to come to me for medicine. He introduced the subject by saying, "O Efendee, do an act of kindness: there are three men poisoned; in your mercy give them medicine, and save their lives:" and then he related the whole affair, without concealing the theft. I answered that they did not deserve medicine; but he urged that by giving it I should obtain an immense reward. "Yes," said I; "'he who saveth a soul alive shall be as if he had saved the lives of all mankind.'"[1] I said this to try the feeling of the applicant, who, expressing admiration of my knowledge, urged me to be quick, lest the men should die; thus showing himself to be no unconditional fatalist. I gave him three strong doses of tartar emetic; and he soon came back to thank me, saying that the medicine was most admirable, for the men had hardly swallowed it when they almost vomited their hearts and livers and everything else in their bodies.

[1] Ḳur. v. 35.

From a distrust in fate some Muslims even shut themselves up during the prevalence of plague; but this practice is generally condemned. A Syrian friend of mine who did so nearly had his door broken open by his neighbours. Another of my friends, one of the most distinguished of the 'Ulamà, confessed to me his conviction of the lawfulness of quarantine and argued well in favour of it; but said that he dared not openly avow such an opinion. "The Apostle of God," said he, "God favour and preserve him! hath commanded that we should not enter a city where there is pestilence, nor go out from it. Why did he say, 'Enter it not'?—because, by so doing, we should expose ourselves to the disease. Why did he say, 'Go not out from it?'—because, by so doing, we should carry the disease to others. The Prophet was tenderly considerate of our welfare: but the present Muslims in general are like bulls [brute beasts]; and they hold the meaning of this command to be, Go not into a city where there is pestilence, because this would be rashness; and go not out from it, because this would be distrusting God's power to save you from it."

Many of the vulgar and ignorant among modern Muslims, believe that the unchangeable destinies of every man are written upon his head, in what are termed the sutures of the skull.

II. The principal Ritual and Moral Laws are on

the following subjects, of which the first four are the most important.

1. Prayer (eṣ-ṣaláh) including preparatory purifications. There are partial or total washings to be performed on particular occasions which need not be described. The ablution which is more especially preparatory to prayer (and which is called wuḍoo) consists in washing the hands, mouth, nostrils, face, arms (as high as the elbow, the right first), each three times; and then the upper part of the head, the beard, ears, neck, and feet, each once. This is done with running water, or from a very large tank, or from a lake, or the sea.

Prayers are required to be performed five times in the course of every day; between daybreak and sunrise, between noon and the 'aṣr, (which latter period is about mid-time between noon and nightfall), between the 'aṣr and sunset, between sunset and the 'eshè (or the period when the darkness of night commences), and at, or after, the 'eshè. The commencement of each of these periods is announced by a chant (called adán), repeated by a crier (muëddin) from the mádineh, or minaret, of each mosque; and it is more meritorious to commence the prayer then than at a later time. On each of these occasions, the Muslim has to perform certain prayers held to be ordained by God, and others ordained by the Prophet; each kind consisting of two, three, or four "rek'ahs;" which term signifies the repetition of a set form of words, chiefly from the Ḳur-án, and ejaculations of "God is most Great!" etc., accompanied by particular postures; part of the words being repeated in an erect posture; part, sitting; and part, in other postures: an inclination of the head and body, followed by two prostrations, distinguishing each rek'ah.[1] These prayers may in some cases be abridged, and in others entirely omitted. Other prayers must be performed on particular occasions.

On Friday, the Mohammadan Sabbath, there are congregational prayers, which are similar to those of others days, with additional prayers and exhortations by a minister, who is called Imám, or Khaṭeeb. The Selám (or Salutation) of Friday—a form of blessing on the Prophet and his family and companions,—is chanted by the muëddins from the mádinehs of the congregational mosques half-an-hour before noon. The worshippers begin to assemble in the mosque as soon as they hear it, and arranging themselves in rows parallel to, and facing, that side in which is the niche that marks the direction of Mekkeh, each performs by himself the prayers of two rek'ahs, which are supererogatory, and then sits in his place while a reader recites part or the whole of the 18th chapter of the Ḳur-án. At the call of noon, they all stand up, and each again performs separately the prayers of two rek'ahs ordained

[1] For a fuller account of the prayers, see "Modern Egyptians," ch. iii.

by the Prophet. A minister standing at the foot of the pulpit-stairs then proposes to bless the Prophet: and accordingly a second Selám is chanted by one or more other ministers stationed on an elevated platform. After this, the former minister, and the latter after him, repeat the call of noon (which the muëddins have before chanted from the mádinehs); and the former enjoins silence. The Khaṭeeb has already seated himself on the top step or platform of the pulpit. He now rises and recites a khuṭbeh of praise to God and exhortation to the congregation; and, if in a country or town acquired by arms from unbelievers, he holds a wooden sword, resting its point on the ground. Each of the congregation next offers up some private supplication; after which, the Khaṭeeb recites a second khuṭbeh, which is always the same or nearly so, in part resembling the first, but chiefly a prayer for the Prophet and his family, and for the general welfare of the Muslims. This finished, the Khateeb descends from the pulpit, and, stationed before the niche, after a form of words[1] differing slightly from the call to prayer has been chanted by the ministers on the elevated platform before mentioned, recites the divinely-ordained prayers of Friday (two rek'ahs) while the people do the same silently, keeping time with him exactly in the various postures. Thus are completed the Friday-prayers; but some of the congregation remain,

[1] The Iḳámeh: see below, ch. viii.

and perform the ordinary divinely-ordained prayers of noon.

Other occasions for special prayer are the two grand annual festivals; the nights of Ramaḍán, the month of abstinence; the occasion of an eclipse of the sun or moon; for rain; previously to the commencement of battle; in pilgrimage; and at funerals.

2. Alms-giving. An alms, called "zekáh," is required by law to be given annually, to the poor, of camels, oxen (bulls and cows) and buffaloes, sheep and goats, horses and mules and asses, and gold and silver (whether in money or in vessels, ornaments, etc.), provided the property be of a certain amount, as five camels, thirty oxen, forty sheep, five horses, two hundred dirhems, or twenty deenárs. The proportion is generally one-fortieth, which is to be paid in kind or in money or other equivalent.

3. Fasting (eṣ-Ṣiyám). The Muslim must abstain from eating and drinking, and from every indulgence of the senses, every day during the month of Ramaḍán, from the first appearance of daybreak until sunset, unless physically incapacitated.—On the first day of the following month, a festival, called the Minor Festival, is observed with public prayer and with general rejoicing, which continues three days.

4. Pilgrimage (el-Ḥájj). It is incumbent on the Muslim, if able, to perform at least once in his life the pilgrimage to Mekkeh and Mount 'Arafát. The

principal ceremonies of the pilgrimage are completed on the 9th of the month of Dhu-l-Ḥijjeh: on the following day, which is the first of the Great Festival, on the return from 'Arafát to Mekkeh, the pilgrims who are able to do so perform a sacrifice, and every other Muslim who can is required to do the same: part of the meat of the victim he should eat, and the rest he should give to the poor. This festival is otherwise observed in a similar manner to the minor one, above mentioned; and lasts three or four days.

The less important ritual and moral laws may here be briefly mentioned.[1]—One of these is circumcision, which is not absolutely obligatory.—The distinctions of clean and unclean meats are nearly the same in the Mohammadan as in the Mosaic code. Camel's flesh is an exception; being lawful to the Muslim. Swine's flesh, and blood, are especially condemned; and a particular mode of slaughtering animals for food is enjoined, accompanied by the repetition of the name of God.—Wine and all inebriating liquors are strictly forbidden.—So too is gaming.—Music is condemned; but most Muslims take great delight in hearing it.—Images and pictures representing living creatures are contrary to law.—Charity, probity in all transactions, veracity (excepting

[1] [For the collected legislation of the Ḳur-án, see my "Speeches and Tabletalk of the Prophet Moḥammad," 133 ff. S. L-P.]

in a few cases),[1] and modesty, are virtues indispensable.—Cleanliness in person, and decent attire, are particularly required. Clothes of silk and ornaments of gold or silver are forbidden to men, but allowed to women: this precept, however, is often disregarded.—Utensils of gold and silver are also condemned: yet they are used by many Muslims.—The manners of Muslims in society are subject to particular rules with respect to salutations, etc.

Of the Civil Laws, the following notices will suffice.—A man may have four wives at the same time, and according to common opinion as many concubine slaves as he pleases.—He may divorce a

[1] Among a people by whom falsehood, in certain cases, is not only allowed but commended, oaths of different kinds are more or less binding. In considering this subject we should also remember that oaths may sometimes be expiated. There are some oaths which, I believe, few Muslims would falsely take; such as saying, three times, "By God the Great!" (Wa-lláhi-l-'aẓeem), and the oath upon the muṣḥaf (or copy of the Ḳur-án), saying, "By what this contains of the word of God!" This latter is rendered more binding by placing a sword with the sacred volume, and still more so by the addition of a cake, or piece, of bread, and a handful of salt. But a form of oath which is generally yet more to be depended upon is that of saying, "I impose upon myself divorcement!" (that is, "the divorce of my wife, if what I say be false"); or, "I impose upon myself interdiction!" which has a similar meaning ("My wife be unlawful to me!"); or, "I impose upon myself a triple divorcement" which binds a man by the irrevocable divorce of his wife. If a man use any of these three forms of oath falsely, his wife, if he have but one, is divorced by the oath itself, if proved to be false, without the absolute necessity of any further ceremony; and if he have two or more wives, he must under such circumstances choose one of them to put away.

wife twice, and each time take her back again; but if he divorce her a third time, or by a triple sentence, he cannot make her his wife again unless by her own consent and by a new contract, and after another man has consummated a marriage with her and divorced her.—The children by a wife and those by a concubine slave inherit equally, if the latter be acknowledged by the father. Sons inherit equally: and so do daughters; but the share of a daughter is half that of a son. One-eighth is the share of the wife or wives of the deceased if he have left issue, and one-fourth if he have left no issue. A husband inherits one-fourth of his wife's property if she have left issue, and one-half if she have left no issue. The debts and legacies of the deceased must first be paid. A man may leave one-third [but no more] of his property in any way he pleases.—When a concubine slave has borne a child to her master, she becomes entitled to freedom on his death. —There are particular laws relating to commerce. Usury and monopoly are especially condemned.

Of the Criminal Laws, a few may be briefly mentioned. Murder is punishable by death, or by a fine to be paid to the family of the deceased, if they prefer it.—Theft, if the property stolen amount to a quarter of a deenár, is to be punished by cutting off the right hand, except under certain circumstances.—Adultery, if attested by four eye-witnesses, is punishable by death (stoning): fornication, by a hundred stripes, and banishment for a year.—Drunkenness is punished with eighty stripes.—Apostasy, persevered in, by death.

The Ḳur-án ordains that murder shall be punished with death; or, rather, that the free shall die for the free, the slave for the slave, and the woman for the woman;[1] or that the perpetrator of the crime shall pay, to the heirs of the person whom he has killed, if they will allow it, a fine, which is to be divided according to the laws of inheritance already explained. It also ordains that unintentional homicide shall be expiated by freeing a believer from slavery, and paying a fine to the family of the person killed, unless they remit it. But these laws are amplified and explained by the same book and by the Imáms. A fine is not to be accepted for murder unless the crime has been attended by some palliating circumstance. This fine, the price of blood, is a hundred camels; or a thousand deenárs (about £500) from him who possesses gold; or, from him who possesses silver, twelve thousand dirhems (about £300). This is for killing a free man; for a woman, half that sum; for a slave, his or her value, but this must fall short of the price of blood for the free. A person unable to free a believer must fast two months as in Ramaḍán. The accomplices of a murderer are liable to the punish-

[1] [But see my "Speeches and Tabletalk of the Prophet Moḥammad," 139, S. L-P.]

ment of death. By the Sunneh (or Traditions of the Prophet) also, a man is obnoxious to capital punishment for the murder of a woman; and by the Ḥanafee law, for the murder of another man's slave. But he is exempted from this punishment who kills his own child or other descendant, or his own slave, or his son's slave, or a slave of whom he is part-owner; so also are his accomplices: and according to Esh-Sháfi'ee, a Muslim, though a slave, is not to be put to death for killing an infidel, though the latter be free. A man who kills another in self-defence, or to defend his property from a robber, is exempt from all punishment. The price of blood is a debt incumbent on the family, tribe, or association, of which the homicide is a member. It is also incumbent on the inhabitants of an enclosed quarter, or the proprietor or proprietors of a field, in which the body of a person killed by an unknown hand is found; unless the person has been found killed in his own house.

Retaliation for intentional wounds and mutilations is allowed by the Mohammadan law, like as for murder, "an eye for an eye," etc.;[1] but a fine may be accepted instead, which the law allows also for unintentional injuries. The fine for a member that is single (as the nose) is the whole price of blood, as for homicide; for a member of which there are two, and not more (as a hand), half the price of blood; for one of which

[1] Ḳur. v. 49.

there are ten (a finger or toe), a tenth of the price of blood: but the fine of a man for maiming or wounding a woman is half of that for the same injury to a man; and that of a free person for injuring a slave varies according to the value of the slave. The fine for depriving a man of any of his five senses, or dangerously wounding him, or grievously disfiguring him for life, is the whole price of blood.

The Mohammadan law ordains that a person who is adult and of sound mind, if he steals an article of the value of a quarter of a deenár (or piece of gold) from a place to which he has not ordinary or free access, shall lose his right hand; but this punishment is not to be inflicted for stealing a free child, or anything which, in the eye of the law, is of no pecuniary value, as wine, or a musical instrument; and there are some other cases in which the thief is not to be so punished. For the second offence, the left foot is to be cut off; and for the third and subsequent offences, according to the Ḥanafee code, the culprit is to be punished by a long imprisonment; or, by the Sháfi'ee law, for the third offence, he is to lose his left hand; for the fourth, his right foot; and for further offences, he is to be flogged or beaten. The punishment is the same for a woman as for a man. This law induced a freethinking Muslim to ask, "If the hand is worth five hundred deenárs [this being the fine for depriving a man of that member], why should it be cut off for a quarter of a deenár?" He was answered, "An honest hand is of great value; but not so is the hand that hath stolen." Amputation for theft, however, is now seldom practised: beating, or some other punishment, is usually inflicted in its stead for the first, second, and third offence; and frequently, death for the fourth.

The Muslims observe two grand 'Eeds or Festivals in every year. The first of these immediately follows Ramaḍán, the month of abstinence, and lasts three days: it is called the Minor Festival. The other, which is called the Great Festival, commences on the tenth of Dhu-l-Ḥijjeh, the day when the pilgrims, halting in the Valley of Minè, on their return from Mount 'Arafát to Mekkeh, perform their sacrifice: the observance of this festival also continues three days, or four.

Early in the first morning, on each of these festivals, the Muslim is required to perform a lustration of his whole person, as on the mornings of Friday; and on the first morning of the Minor Festival he should break his fast with a few dates or some other light food, but on the Great Festival he abstains from food until he has acquitted himself of the religious duties now to be mentioned. Soon after sunrise on the first day of each festival, the men, dressed in new or in their best clothes, repair to the mosque or to a particular place appointed for the performance of the prayers of the 'Eed. On going thither, they should repeat frequently "God is most Great!"—on the Minor Festival inaudibly, on the other aloud. The congregation having assembled repeat the prayers of two rek'ahs; after which the Khaṭeeb recites a khuṭbeh, *i.e.* an exhortation and a prayer. On each of these festivals, in the mosque or place of prayer and in the street and at each other's houses, friends congratulate and embrace one another, generally paying visits for this purpose; and the great receive visits from their dependants. The young on these occasions kiss the right hand of the aged, and servants or dependants do the same to their masters or superiors, unless the latter be of high rank, in which case they kiss the end of the hanging sleeves or the skirt of the outer garment. Most of the shops are closed, excepting those at which eatables and sweet drinks are sold; but the streets are filled with people in their holiday-clothes.

On the Minor Festival, which, as it terminates an arduous fast, is celebrated with more rejoicing than the other,[1] servants and other dependants receive presents of new articles of clothing from their masters or patrons; and the servant receives presents of small sums of money from his master's friends, whom, if they

[1] Hence it has been called, by many travellers, and even by some learned Orientalists, the Great Feast; but it is never so called by the Arabs.

do not visit his master, he goes to congratulate; as well as from any former master, to whom he often takes a plate-full of kaḥks. These are sweet cakes or biscuits of an annular form, composed of flower and butter, with a little 'ajameeyeh (a thick paste consisting of butter, honey, a little flour, and some spices) inside. They are also often sent as presents on this occasion by other people. Another custom required of the faithful on this festival is the giving of alms.

On the Great Festival, after the prayers of the congregation, every one who can afford it performs, with his own hand or by that of a deputy, a sacrifice of a ram, he-goat, cow or buffalo, or she-camel; part of the meat of which he eats, and part he gives to the poor, or to his friends or dependants. The ram or goat should be at least one year old; the cow or buffalo, two years; and the camel, five years; and none should have any considerable mutilation or infirmity. A cow or buffalo, or a camel, is a sufficient sacrifice for seven persons. The clothes which were put on new at the former festival are generally worn on this occasion; and the presents which are given to servants and others are usually somewhat less.

On each of the two festivals it is also customary, especially with the women, to visit the tombs of relations. The party generally take with them a palm-branch, and place it, broken in several pieces, or merely its leaves, upon the tomb or monument; or some, instead of this, place sweet basil or other flowers. They also usually provide themselves with sweet cakes, bread, dates, or some other kind of food, to distribute to the poor. But their first duty on arriving at the tomb is to recite the Fátiḥah (the opening chapter of the Ḳur-án), or to employ a person to recite previously a longer chapter, generally the thirty-sixth (Soorat Yá-Seen), or even the whole of the book: sometimes the visitors recite the Fátiḥah, and, after having hired a person to perform a longer recitation, go away before he commences. The women often stay all the days of the festivals in the cemeteries, either in tents or in houses of their own erected there for their reception on these and other occasions. The tent of each party surrounds the tomb which is the object of their visit. In the outskirts of the cemeteries, swings and whirligigs are set up, and story-tellers, jugglers, and dancers amuse the populace.

CHAPTER II.

DEMONOLOGY.

The Muslims, in general, believe in three different species of created intelligent beings: Angels, who are created of light; Genii, who are created of fire; and Men, created of earth. The first species are called Meláïkeh (sing. Melek); the second, Jinn (sing. Jinnee); the third, Ins (sing. Insee). Some hold that the Devils (Sheyṭáns) are of a species distinct from Angels and Jinn; but the more prevailing opinion, and that which rests on the highest authority, is, that they are rebellious Jinn.

"It is believed," says El-Ḳazweenee, "that the Angels are of a simple substance, endowed with life and speech and reason, and that the difference between them and the Jinn and Sheyṭáns is a difference of species. Know," he adds, "that the Angels are sanctified from carnal desire and the disturbance of anger: they disobey not God in what He hath commanded them, but do what they are commanded. Their food is the celebrating of his glory; their drink, the proclaiming of his holiness; their conversation, the commemoration of God, whose name be exalted; their pleasure, his worship; they are created in different forms, and with different powers." Some are described as having the forms of brutes. Four of them are Archangels; Jebraeel or Jibreel (Gabriel), the angel of revelations; Meekaeel or Meekál (Michael), the patron of the Israelites; 'Azraeel, the angel of death; and Isráfeel, the angel of the trumpet, which he is to sound twice, or as some say thrice, at the end of the world—one blast will kill all living creatures (himself included), another, forty years after, (he being raised again for this purpose, with Jebraeel and Meekaeel,) will raise the dead. These Archangels are also called Apostolic Angels. They are inferior in dignity to human prophets and apostles, though superior to the rest of the human race: the angelic nature is held to be inferior to the human nature, because all the Angels were commanded to prostrate themselves before Adam. Every believer is attended by two guardian and recording angels, one of whom writes his good actions, the other, his evil actions: or, according to some, the number of these angels is five, or sixty, or a hundred and sixty. There are also two Angels, called Munkir (vulg. Nákir) and Nekeer, who examine all the dead and torture the wicked in their graves.

The species of Jinn is said to have been created some thousands of years before Adam. According to a tradition from the Prophet, this species consists of five orders or classes; namely, Jánn (who are the least powerful of all), Jinn, Sheyṭáns (or Devils), 'Efreets, and Márids. The last, it is added, are the most powerful; and the Jánn are transformed Jinn, like as certain apes and swine were transformed men.[1]—It must, however, be remarked here that the terms Jinn and Jánn are generally used indiscriminately as names of the whole species (including the other orders above mentioned), whether good or bad; and that the former term is the more common; also, that Sheyṭán is commonly used to signify any evil Jinnee. An 'Efreet is a powerful evil Jinnee: a Márid, an evil Jinnee of the most powerful class. The Jinn (but, generally speaking, evil ones) are called by the Persians Deevs; the most powerful evil Jinn, Narahs (which signifies "males," though they are said to be males and females); the good Jinn, Perees, though this term is commonly applied to females.

In a tradition from the Prophet, it is said, "The Jánn were created of a smokeless fire."[2] El-Jánn is sometimes used as a name of Iblees, as in the following verse of the Ḳur-án:—"And the Jánn [the father of

[1] Mir-át ez-Zemán (MS. in my possession)—a great history whose author lived in the thirteenth century of our era. See also Ḳur. v. 65.

[2] Mir-át ez-Zemán. Ḳur. lv. 14. The word which signifies "a smokeless fire" has been misunderstood by some as meaning "the flame of fire:" El-Jóheree (in the Ṣiḥáḥ) renders it rightly; and says that of this fire was *the* Sheyṭán (Iblees) created.

the Jinn; *i.e.* Iblees] we had created before [*i.e.* before the creation of Adam] of the fire of the samoom [*i.e.* of fire without smoke]."[1] Jánn also signifies "a serpent," as in other passages of the Ḳur-án;[2] and is used in the same book as synonymous with Jinn.[3] In the last sense it is generally believed to be used in the tradition quoted in the commencement of this paragraph. There are several apparently contradictory traditions from the Prophet which are reconciled by what has been above stated: in one, it is said, that Iblees was the father of all the Jánn and Sheyṭáns,[4] Jánn being here synonymous with Jinn; in another, that Jánn was the father of all the Jinn,[5] Jánn being here used as a name of Iblees.

"It is held," says El-Ḳazweenee, a writer of the thirteenth century, "that the Jinn are aërial animals, with transparent bodies, which can assume various forms. People differ in opinion respecting these beings: some consider the Jinn and Sheyṭáns as unruly men, but these persons are of the Moạtezileh [a sect of Muslim freethinkers]; and some hold that God, whose name be exalted, created the Angels of the light of fire, and the Jinn of its flame [but this is at variance with the general opinion], and the Sheyṭáns of its

[1] Ḳur. xv. 27; and Commentary of the Jeláleyn.
[2] Ḳur. xxvii. 10; and xxviii. 31; and the Jeláleyn.
[3] Ḳur. lv. 39, 74; and the Jeláleyn.
[4] 'Ikrimeh, from Ibn-'Abbás, in the Mir-át ez-Zemán.
[5] Mujáhid, from the same, ibid.

smoke [which is also at variance with the common opinion], and that [all] these kinds of beings are [usually] invisible[1] to men, but that they assume what forms they please, and when their form becomes condensed they are visible."—This last remark illustrates several descriptions of Jinnees in the "Thousand and One Nights," where the form of the monster is at first undefined, or like an enormous pillar, and then gradually assumes a human shape and less gigantic size.

It is said that God created the Jánn (or Jinn) two thousand years before Adam (or, according to some writers, much earlier), and that there are believers and infidels, and every sect, among them, as among men.[2] Some say that a prophet, named Yoosuf, was sent to the Jinn; others, that they had only preachers or admonishers; others, again, that seventy apostles were sent, before Moḥammad, to Jinn and men conjointly.[3] It is commonly believed that the preadamite Jinn were governed by forty (or, according to some, seventy-two) kings, to each of whom the Arab writers give the name of Suleymán (Solomon); and that they derive their appellation from the last of these, who was called Jánn Ibn Jánn, and who, some say, built the Pyramids of Egypt. The following account of the preadamite Jinn is given by El-Ḳazweenee.—"It is related in histories that a race of Jinn in ancient

[1] Hence the appellations of "Jinn" and "Jánn."

[2] Tradition from the Prophet, in the Mir-át ez-Zemán. [3] Ibid.

times, before the creation of Adam, inhabited the earth and covered it, the land and the sea, and the plains and the mountains; and the favours of God were multiplied upon them, and they had government and prophecy and religion and law. But they transgressed and offended, and opposed their prophets, and made wickedness to abound in the earth; whereupon God, whose name be exalted, sent against them an army of Angels, who took possession of the earth, and drove away the Jinn to the regions of the islands, and made many of them prisoners; and of those who were made prisoners was 'Azázeel [afterwards called Iblees, from his *despair*]; and a slaughter was made among them. At that time, 'Azázeel was young: he grew up among the Angels [and probably for that reason was called one of them], and became learned in their knowledge, and assumed the government of them; and his days were prolonged until he became their chief; and thus it continued for a long time, until the affair between him and Adam happened, as God, whose name be exalted, hath said, 'When we said unto the Angels, Worship[1] ye Adam, and [all] worshipped except Iblees, [who] was [one] of the Jinn.'"[2]

"Iblees," we are told by another author, "was sent as a governor upon the earth, and judged among the Jinn a thousand years, after which he ascended into

[1] The worship here spoken of is prostration, as an act of obeisance to a superior being.

[2] Ḳur. xviii. 48.

heaven, and remained employed in worship until the creation of Adam."[1] The name of Iblees was originally, according to some, 'Azázeel (as before mentioned); and according to others, El-Ḥárith: his patronymic is Aboo-Murrah, or Abu-l-Ghimr.[2] It is disputed whether he was of the Angels or of the Jinn. There are three opinions on this point.—1. That he was of the Angels, from a tradition from Ibn-'Abbás. —2. That he was of the Sheyṭáns (or evil Jinn); as it is said in the Ḳur-án, "except Iblees, [who] was [one] of the Jinn:" this was the opinion of El-Ḥasan El-Baṣree, and is that commonly held.—3. That he was neither of the Angels nor of the Jinn; but created alone, of fire. Ibn-'Abbás founds his opinion on the same text from which El-Ḥasan El-Baṣree derives his: "When we said unto the Angels, Worship ye Adam, and [all] worshipped except Iblees, [who] was [one] of the Jinn" (before quoted): which he explains by saying, that the most noble and honourable among the Angels are called "the Jinn," because they are *veiled* from the eyes of the other Angels on account of their superiority; and that Iblees was one of these Jinn. He adds that he had the government of the lowest heaven and of the earth, and was called the Ṭáoos (literally, Peacock) of the Angels; and that there was not a spot in the lowest heaven but he had

[1] Eṭ-Ṭabaree, quoted in the Mir-át ez-Zemán.
[2] Mir-át ez-Zemán.

prostrated himself upon it: but when the Jinn rebelled upon the earth, God sent a troop of Angels who drove them to the islands and mountains; and Iblees being elated with pride, and refusing to prostrate himself before Adam, God transformed him into a Sheyṭán. But this reasoning is opposed by other verses, in which Iblees is represented as saying, "Thou hast created *me* of *fire*, and hast created *him* [Adam] of earth."[1] It is therefore argued, "If he were created originally of fire, how was he created of light? for the Angels were [all] created of light."[2] The former verse may be explained by the tradition that Iblees, having been taken captive, was exalted among the Angels; or perhaps there is an ellipsis after the word "Angels;" for it might be inferred that the command given to the Angels was also (and *à fortiori*) to be obeyed by the Jinn.

According to a tradition, Iblees and all the Sheyṭáns are distinguished from the other Jinn by a longer existence. "The Sheyṭáns," it is added, "are the children of Iblees, and die not but with him, whereas the [other] Jinn die before him;"[3] though they may live many centuries. But this is not altogether accordant with the popular belief: Iblees and many other evil Jinn are to survive mankind, but they are

[1] Ḳur. vii. 11; and xxxviii. 77.

[2] Mir-át ez-Zemán.

[3] El-Ḥasan El-Baṣree, in the Mir-át ez-Zemán. My interpolation of the word "other" is required by his opinion before stated.

to die before the general resurrection, as also even the Angels, the last of whom will be the Angel of Death, 'Azraeel. Yet not *all* the evil Jinn are to live thus long: many of them are killed by shooting stars, hurled at them from heaven; wherefore, the Arabs, when they see a shooting star (shiháb), often exclaim, "May God transfix the enemy of the faith!" Many also are killed by other Jinn, and some even by men. The fire of which the Jinnee is created circulates in his veins, in place of blood: therefore, when he receives a mortal wound, this fire, issuing from his veins, generally consumes him to ashes.

The Jinn, it has been already shown, are peccable. They eat and drink, and propagate their species, sometimes in conjunction with human beings; in which latter case, the offspring partakes of the nature of both parents. In all these respects they differ from the Angels. Among the evil Jinn are distinguished the five sons of their chief, Iblees; namely, Teer, who brings about calamities, losses and injuries; El-Aạwar, who encourages debauchery; Sóṭ, who suggests lies; Dásim, who causes hatred between man and wife; and Zelemboor, who presides over places of traffic.[1]

The most common forms and habitations or places of resort of the Jinn must now be described.

The following traditions from the Prophet are the

[1] Mujáhid, quoted by El-Ḳazweenee.

most to the purpose that I have seen.—The Jinn are of various shapes; having the forms of serpents, scorpions, lions, wolves, jackals, etc.[1] The Jinn are of three kinds: one on the land, one in the sea, and one in the air.[2] The Jinn consist of forty troops; each troop consisting of six hundred thousand.[3]—The Jinn are of three kinds: one have wings and fly; another are snakes and dogs; and the third move about from place to place like men.[4] Domestic snakes are asserted to be Jinn on the same authority.[5]

The Prophet ordered his followers to kill serpents and scorpions if they intruded at prayers; but on other occasions he seems to have required first to admonish them to depart, and then, if they remained, to kill them. The Doctors, however, differ in opinion whether *all* kinds of snakes or serpents should be admonished first, or whether *any* should; for the Prophet, say they, took a covenant of the Jinn [probably after the above-mentioned command], that they should not enter the houses of the faithful: therefore, it is argued, if they enter, they break their covenant, and it becomes lawful to kill them without previous warning. Yet it is related that 'Aïsheh, the Prophet's wife, having killed a serpent

[1] Mujáhid, from Ibn-'Abbás, in the Mir-át ez-Zemán.

[2] El-Ḥasan El-Baṣree, ibid.

[3] 'Ikrimeh, from Ibn-'Abbás, ibid.

[4] Mishkát el-Maṣábeeḥ, ii. 314.

[5] Ibid. ii. 311, 312.

in her chamber, was alarmed by a dream, and fearing that it might have been a Muslim Jinnee, as it did not enter her chamber when she was undressed, gave in alms, as an expiation, twelve thousand dirhems (about £300), the price of the blood of a Muslim.[1]

The Jinn were said to appear to mankind most commonly in the shapes of serpents, dogs, cats, or human beings. In the last case, they are sometimes of the stature of men, and sometimes of a size enormously gigantic. If good, they are generally resplendently handsome: if evil, horribly hideous. They become invisible at pleasure, by a rapid extension or rarefaction of the particles which compose them, or suddenly disappear in the earth or air or through a solid wall. Many Muslims in the present day profess to have seen and held intercourse with them:—witness the following anecdote, which was related to me by a Persian with whom I was acquainted in Cairo, named Abu-l-Ḳásim, a native of Jeelán, then superintendent of Moḥammad 'Alee's Printing-office at Booláḳ.

One of this person's countrymen, whom he asserted to be a man of indubitable veracity, was sitting on the roof of a house which he had hired, overlooking the Ganges, and was passing the closing hour of the day, according to his usual custom, in smoking his Persian pipe and feasting his eyes by gazing at the beautiful

[1] Mir-át ez-Zemán. See above, p. 18.

forms of Indian maidens bathing in the river, when he beheld among them one so lovely that his heart was overpowered with desire to have her for his wife. At nightfall she came to him, and told him that she had observed his emotion and would consent to become his wife; but on the condition that he should never admit another female to take or share her place, and that she should only be with him in the night time. They took the marriage-vow to each other, with none for their witness but God; and great was his happiness, till, one evening, he saw again, among a group of girls in the river, another who excited in him still more powerful emotions. To his surprise, this very form stood before him at the approach of night. He withstood the temptation, mindful of his marriage-vow; she used every allurement, but he was resolute. His fair visitor then told him that she was his wife; that she was a jinneeyeh; and that she would always thenceforward visit him in the form of any females whom he might chance to desire.

The Zóba'ah, which is a whirlwind that raises the sand or dust in the form of a pillar of prodigious height, often seen sweeping across the deserts and fields, is believed to be caused by the flight of an evil Jinnee. To defend themselves from a Jinnee thus "riding in the whirlwind," the Arabs often exclaim, "Iron! Iron!" (Ḥadeed! Ḥadeed!), or, "Iron! thou unlucky!" (Ḥadeed! yá mashoom!) as the Jinn are supposed to have a great dread of that metal: or they exclaim, "God is most great!" (Alláhu akbar!).[1] A similar superstition prevails with respect to the water-spout at sea, as may be seen in the adventures of King Shahriyár in the introduction to the "Thousand and One Nights."

It is believed that the chief abode of the Jinn is in the Mountains of Ḳáf, which are supposed to encompass the whole of our earth. But they are also believed to pervade the solid body of our earth, and the firmament; and to choose as their principal places of resort or of occasional abode, baths, wells, ovens, ruined houses, market-places, the junctures of roads, the sea, and rivers. The Arabs, therefore, when they pour water on the ground, or enter a bath, or let down a bucket into a well, and on various other occasions, say "Permission! or "Permission, ye blessed!" (Destoor! or Destoor yá mubárakeen![2]) The evil spirits (or evil Jinn), it is said, had liberty to enter any of the seven heavens till the birth of Jesus, when they were excluded from three of them: on the birth of Moḥammad they were forbidden the other four.[3] They continue, however, to ascend to the confines of the lowest heaven, and there listening to the conversation of the Angels respecting things decreed by God, obtain knowledge of futurity, which they some-

[1] Modern Egyptians, ch. x. [2] Ibid.

[3] Sale, in a note on chap. xv. of the Ḳur-án.

times impart to men, who, by means of talismans, or certain invocations, make them to serve the purposes of magical performances. What the Prophet said of Iblees, in the following tradition, applies also to the evil Jinn over whom he presides:—His chief abode [among men] is the bath; his chief places of resort are the markets, and the junctures of roads; his food is whatever is killed without the name of God being pronounced over it; his drink, whatever is intoxicating; his muëddin, the mizmár (a musical pipe, *i.e.* any musical instrument); his Ḳur-án, poetry; his written character, the marks made in geomancy;[1] his speech, falsehood; his snares, women.[2]

That particular Jinn presided over particular places was an opinion of the early Arabs. It is said in the Ḳur-án, "And there were certain men who sought refuge with certain of the Jinn."[3] In the Commentary of the Jeláleyn, I find the following remark on these words:—"When they halted on their journey in a place of fear, each man said, 'I seek refuge with the lord of this place, from the mischief of his foolish ones!'" In illustration of this, I may insert the following tradition, translated from El-Ḳazweenee:—"It is related by a certain narrator of

[1] So I translate the word "khaṭṭ;" but in Es-Suyooṭee's Nuzhet el-Mutaämmil wa-Murshid el-Mutaähhil, section 7, I find, in its place, the word "weshm," or "tattooing;" and there are some other slight variations and omissions in this tradition as there quoted.

[2] El-Ḳazweenee.

[3] Ḳur. lxxii. 6.

traditions, that he descended into a valley with his sheep, and a wolf carried off a ewe from among them; and he arose, and raised his voice, and cried, 'O inhabitant of the valley!' whereupon he heard a voice saying, 'O wolf, restore to him his sheep!' and the wolf came with the ewe, and left her and departed." The same opinion is held by the modern Arabs, though probably they do not use such an invocation. A similar superstition, a relic of ancient Egyptian credulity, still prevails among the people of Cairo. It is believed that each quarter of this city has its peculiar guardian-genius, or Agathodaemon, which has the form of a serpent.[1]

It has already been mentioned that some of the Jinn are Muslims, and others infidels. The good Jinn acquit themselves of the imperative duties of religion, namely, prayers, alms-giving, fasting during the month of Ramaḍán, and pilgrimage to Mekkeh and Mount 'Arafát; but in the performance of these duties they are generally invisible to human beings.[2]

It has been stated, that, by means of talismans, or certain invocations, men are said to obtain the services of Jinn; and the manner in which the latter are enabled to assist magicians, by imparting to them the knowledge of future events, has been explained above. No man ever obtained such absolute power over the Jinn as Suleymán Ibn Dáood (Solomon, the son of David).

[1] Modern Egyptians, ch. x. [2] Ibid. ch. xxiv.

This he did by virtue of a most wonderful talisman, which is said to have come down to him from heaven. It was a seal-ring, upon which was engraved "the most great name" of God, and was partly composed of brass and partly of iron. With the brass he stamped his written commands to the good Jinn; with the iron (for the reason before mentioned, p. 36), those to the evil Jinn or Devils. Over both orders he had unlimited power; as well as over the birds and the winds,[1] and, as is generally said, over the wild beasts. His Wezeer, Áṣaf the son of Barkhiyà, is also said to have been acquainted with "the most great name," by uttering which, the greatest miracles may be performed,—even that of raising the dead. By virtue of this name engraved on his ring, Suleymán compelled the Jinn to assist in building the Temple of Jerusalem, and in various other works. Many of the evil Jinn he converted to the true faith, and many others of this class, who remained obstinate in infidelity, he confined in prisons. He is said to have been monarch of the whole earth. Hence, perhaps, the name of Suleymán is given to the universal monarchs of the preadamite Jinn; unless the story of his own universal dominion originated from confounding him with those kings.

The injuries related to have been inflicted upon human beings by evil Jinn are of various kinds. Jinn are said to have often carried off beautiful

[1] Ḳur. xxvii. 17; xxxviii. 35.

women, whom they have forcibly kept as their wives or concubines. Malicious or disturbed Jinn are asserted often to station themselves on the roofs or at the windows of houses, and to throw down bricks and stones on persons passing by. When they take possession of an uninhabited house, they seldom fail to persecute terribly any person who goes to reside in it. They are also very apt to pilfer provisions, etc. Many learned and devout persons, to secure their property from such depredations, repeat the words "In the name of God, the Compassionate, the Merciful!" on locking the doors of their houses, rooms, or closets, and on covering the bread-basket, or anything containing food.[1] During the month of Ramaḍán, the evil Jinn are believed to be confined in prison; and therefore, on the last night of that month, with the same view, women sometimes repeat the words above mentioned, and sprinkle salt upon the floors of the apartments of their houses.[2]

To complete this sketch of Arabian demonology, an account must be added of several creatures generally believed to be of inferior orders of the Jinn.

One of these is the Ghool, which is commonly regarded as a kind of Sheyṭán or evil Jinnee, that eats men; and is also described by some as a Jinnee or an enchanter who assumes various forms. The Ghools are said to appear in the forms of human

[1] Modern Egyptians, ch. x. [2] Ibid.

beings, and of various animals, and in many monstrous shapes; to haunt burial-grounds and other sequestered spots; to feed upon dead human bodies; and to kill and devour any human creature who has the misfortune to fall in their way: whence the term "Ghool" is applied to any cannibal. An opinion quoted by a celebrated author respecting the Ghool is that it is a demoniacal animal, which passes a solitary existence in the deserts, resembling both man and brute; that it appears to a person travelling alone in the night and in solitary places, and being supposed by him to be itself a traveller, lures him out of his way.[1]

Another opinion stated by him is this: that when the Sheyṭáns attempt to hear words by stealth [from the confines of the lowest heaven] they are struck by shooting-stars; and some are burnt; some, falling into a sea, or rather a large river (baḥr), are converted into crocodiles; and some, falling upon the land, become Ghools. The same author adds the following tradition:—"The Ghool is any Jinnee that is opposed to travels, assuming various forms and appearances;"[2] and affirms that several of the Companions of the Prophet saw Ghools in their travels, and that 'Omar, among them, saw a Ghool while on a journey to Syria, before El-Islám, and struck it with his sword. It appears that "Ghool" is, properly speaking, a

[1] El-Ḳazweenee. [2] El-Jáḥiz ('Amr Ibn-Baḥr).

name only given to a *female* demon of the kind above described: the male is called "Ḳuṭrub." It is said that these beings, and the Ghaddár or Gharrár, and other similar creatures which will presently be mentioned, are the offspring of Iblees and of a wife whom God created for him of the fire of the samoom (which here signifies, as in an instance before mentioned, "a smoke-less fire"); and that they sprang from an egg.[1] The female Ghool, it is added, appears to men in the deserts, in various forms, converses with them, and sometimes yields herself to them.

The Seạláh, or Saạláh, is another demoniacal creature, described by most authors as of the Jinn. It is said that it is mostly found in forests; and that when it captures a man, it makes him dance, and plays with him as the cat plays with the mouse. A man of Iṣfahán asserted that many beings of this kind abounded in his country; that sometimes the wolf would hunt one of them by night, and devour it, and that, when it had seized it, the Seạláh would cry out, "Come to my help, for the wolf devoureth me!" or it would cry, "Who will liberate me? I have a hundred deenárs, and he shall receive them!" but the people knowing that it was the cry of the Seạláh, no one would liberate it; and so the wolf would eat it.[2]—An

[1] Tradition from Wahb Ibn-Munebbih, quoted in the account of the early Arabs in the Mir-át ez-Zemán.

[2] El-Ḳazweenee.

island in the sea of Eṣ-Ṣeen (China) is called "the Island of the Seạláh," by Arab geographers, from its being said to be inhabited by the demons so named: they are described as creatures of hideous forms, supposed to be Sheyṭans, the offspring of human beings and Jinn, who eat men.[1]

The Ghaddár, or Gharrár,[2] is another creature of a similar nature, described as being found in the borders of El-Yemen, and sometimes in Tihámeh, and in the upper parts of Egypt. It is said that it entices a man to it, and either tortures him in a manner not to be described, or merely terrifies him, and leaves him.[3]

The Delhán is also a demoniacal being, inhabiting the islands of the seas, having the form of a man, and riding on an ostrich. It eats the flesh of men whom the sea casts on the shore from wrecks. Some say that a Delhán once attacked a ship in the sea, and desired to take the crew; but they contended with it; whereupon it uttered a cry which caused them to fall upon their faces, and it took them.[4]

[1] Ibn-El-Wardee [fifteenth century].

[2] Its name is written differently in two different MSS. in my possession.

[3] El-Ḳazweenee, and Mir-át ez-Zemán.

[4] El-Ḳazweenee. In my MS. of Ibn-El-Wardee, I find the name written "Dahlán." He mentions an island called by this name, in the Sea of 'Omán; and describes its inhabitants as cannibal Sheyṭáns, like men in form, and riding on birds resembling ostriches. There is also an inferior class of the Jinn, termed El-Ghowwáṣah, that is, the Divers or Plungers in the seas.

The Shiḳḳ is another demoniacal creature, having the form of half a human being (like a man divided longitudinally); and it is believed that the Nesnás is the offspring of a Shiḳḳ and of a human being. The former appears to travellers; and it was a demon of this kind who killed, and was killed by, 'Alḳamah, the son of Ṣafwán, the son of Umeiyeh; of whom it is well known that he was killed by a Jinnee. So says El-Ḳazweenee.

The Nesnás (above mentioned) is described as resembling half a human being; having half a head, half a body, one arm, and one leg, with which it hops with much agility; as being found in the woods of El-Yemen, and being endowed with speech: "but God," it is added, "is all-knowing."[1] It is said that it is found in Ḥaḍramót as well as El-Yemen; and that one was brought alive to El-Mutawekkil: it resembled a man in form, excepting that it had but half a face, which was in its breast, and a tail like that of a sheep. The people of Ḥaḍramót, it is added, eat it; and its flesh is sweet. It is only generated in their country. A man who went there asserted that he saw a captured Nesnás, which cried out for mercy, conjuring him by God and by himself.[2] A race of people whose head is in the breast, is described as inhabiting an island called Jábeh (supposed to be Java), in the Sea of El-Hind

[1] El-Ḳazweenee, in the khátimeh [or epilogue] of his work.

[2] Mir-át ez-Zemán.

(India).[1] A kind of Nesnás is also described as inhabiting the Island of Ráïj, in the Sea of Eṣ-Ṣeen (China), and having wings like those of the bat.[2]

The Hátif is a being that is heard, but not seen; and is often mentioned by Arab writers. It is generally the communicator of some intelligence in the way of advice, or direction, or warning.

Here terminating this chapter, I must beg the reader to remark that the superstitious fancies which it describes are prevalent among all classes of the Arabs, and the Muslims in general, learned as well as vulgar.

[1] Ibn-El-Wardee. [2] Idem.

CHAPTER III.

SAINTS.

THE Arabs entertain remarkable opinions with respect to the offices and supernatural powers of their saints, which form an important part of the mysteries of the Darweeshes (Dervishes), and are but imperfectly known to the generality of Muslims.

Muslim Saints and devotees are known by the common appellation of Welees, or particular favourites of God. The more eminent among them compose a mysterious hierarchical body, whose government respects the whole human race, infidels as well as believers, but whose power is often exercised in such a manner that the subjects influenced by it know not from what person or persons its effects proceed. The general governor or coryphaeus of these holy beings is commonly called the Ḳuṭb, which literally signifies a "pole," or an "axis," and is metaphorically used to signify a "chief," either in a civil or political, or in a spiritual sense. The Ḳuṭb of the saints is distinguished by other appellations: he is called Ḳuṭb el-Ghós, or Ḳuṭb el-Ghóth (the Ḳuṭb of Invocation for Help), etc.; and simply, El-Ghós.[1] The orders under the rule of this chief are called 'Omud (or Owtád), Akhyár, Abdál, Nujaba, and Nuḳaba: I name them according to their precedence.[2] Perhaps to these should be added an inferior order called Aṣḥáb ed-Darak, *i.e.* "Watchmen," or "Overseers." The members are not known as such to their inferior unenlightened fellow-creatures, and are often invisible to them. This is more frequently the case with the Ḳuṭb, who, though generally stationed at Mekkeh, on the roof of the Kaạbeh, is never visible there, nor at any of his other favourite stations or places of resort; yet his voice is often heard at these places. Whenever he and the saints under his authority mingle among ordinary men, they are not distinguished by a dignified

[1] D'Ohsson (i. 315, 316) asserts the Ḳuṭb to be the chief minister of the Ghós; and gives an account somewhat different from that which I offer of the orders under his authority: but perhaps the Turkish Darweeshes differ from the Arab in their tenets on this subject.

[2] It is said that "the Nuḳaba are three hundred; the Nujaba, seventy; the Abdál, forty; the Akhyár, seven; the 'Omud, four; the Ghós [as before mentioned], one. The Nuḳaba reside in El-Gharb [Northern Africa to the west of Egypt]; the Nujaba, in Egypt; the Abdál, in Syriạ; the Akhyár travel about the earth; the 'Omud, in the corners of the earth; the abode of the Ghós is at Mekkeh. In an affair of need, the Nuḳaba implore relief for the people; then, the Nujaba; then, the Abdál; then, the Akhyár; then, the 'Omud; and if their prayer be not answered, the Ghós implores, and his prayer is answered." (El-Isḥáḳee's History, preface.)—This statement, I find, rests on the authority of a famous saint of Baghdád Aboo-Bekr El-Kettánee, who died at Mekkeh, in the year of the Flight, 322. (Mir-át ez-Zemán, events of that year).

appearance, but are always humbly clad. These, and even inferior saints, are said to perform astonishing miracles, such as flying in the air, passing unhurt through fire, swallowing fire, glass, etc., walking upon water, transporting themselves in a moment of time to immense distances, and supplying themselves and others with food in desert places. Their supernatural power they are supposed to obtain by a life of the most exalted piety, and especially by constant self-denial, accompanied with the most implicit reliance upon God, by the services of good genii, and, as many believe, by the knowledge and utterance of "the most great name" of God. A miracle performed by a saint is distinguished by the term "karámeh" from one performed by a prophet, which is called "moạjizeh."

El-Khiḍr and Ilyás (Elias), are both believed to have been Ḳuṭbs, and the latter is called in the Ḳur-án an apostle; but it is disputed whether the former was a prophet or merely a welee. Both are said to have drunk of the Fountain of Life, and to be in consequence still living; and Ilyás is commonly believed to invest the successive Ḳuṭbs. The similarity of the miracles ascribed to the Ḳuṭbs to those performed by Elias or Elijah, I have remarked in a former work.[1] Another miracle, reminding us of the mantle of Elijah in the hands of his successor, may here be mentioned.—A

[1] Modern Egyptians, ch. x.

saint who was the Ḳuṭb of his time, dying at Tunis, left his clothes in trust to his attendant, Moḥammad El-Ashwam, a native of the neighbouring regency of Tripoli, who desired to sell these relics, but was counselled to retain them, and accordingly, though high prices were bidden for them, made them his own by purchase. As soon as they became his property, he was affected, we are told, with a divine ecstasy, and endowed with miraculous powers.[1]

Innumerable miracles are related to have been performed by Muslim saints, and large volumes are filled with the histories of their wonderful lives. The author of the work from which the above story is taken, mentions, as a fact to be relied on, in an account of one of his ancestors, that, his lamp happening to go out one night while he was reading alone in the riwáḳ of the Jabart (of which he was the sheykh), in the great mosque El-Azhar, the forefinger of his right hand emitted a light which enabled him to continue his reading until his naḳeeb had trimmed and lighted another lamp.[2]

From many stories of a similar kind that I have

[1] El-Jabartee's History of Modern Egypt, vol. ii., obituary of the year 1201 (MS. in my possession).—The appellation of "the four Ḳuṭbs" is given in Egypt to the seyyid Aḥmad Rifá'ah, the seyyid 'Abd-El-Ḳádir El-Jeelánee, the seyyid Aḥmad El-Bedawee, and the seyyid Ibráheem Ed-Dasooḳee, the founders of the four orders of darweeshes most celebrated among the Arabs, called Rifá'eeyeh, Ḳádireeyeh, Aḥmedeeyeh, and Barábimeh.

[2] El-Jabartee's History, vol. i., obituary of the year 1188.

read, I select the following as a fair specimen: it is related by a very celebrated saint, Ibráheem El-Khowwáṣ.—"I entered the desert [on pilgrimage to Mekkeh from El-'Irák̩], and there joined me a man having a belt round his waist, and I said, 'Who art thou?'—He answered, 'A Christian; and I desire thy company.' We walked together for seven days, eating nothing; after which he said to me, 'O monk of the Muslims, produce what thou hast in the way of refreshment, for we are hungry:' so I said, 'O my God, disgrace me not before this infidel:' and lo, a tray, upon which were bread and broiled meat and fresh dates and a mug of water. We ate, and continued our journey seven days more; and I then said to him, 'O monk of the Christians, produce what thou hast in the way of refreshment; for the turn is come to thee:' whereupon he leaned upon his staff, and prayed; and lo, two trays, containing double that which was on my tray. I was confounded, and refused to eat: he urged me, saying, 'Eat;' but I did it not. Then said he, 'Be glad; for I give thee two pieces of good news: one of them is that I testify that there is no deity but God and that Moḥammad is God's Apostle: the other, that I said, O God, if there be worth in this servant, supply me with two trays:—so this is through thy blessing.' We ate, and the man put on the dress of pilgrimage, and so entered Mekkeh, where he remained with me a year as a student; after which he died, and I buried him in [the cemetery] El-Maạlà." "And God," says the author from whom I take this story, "is all-knowing:" *i.e.* He alone knoweth whether it be strictly true: but this is often added to the narration of traditions resting upon high authority.[1]

The saint above mentioned was called "El-Khowwáṣ" (or the maker of palm-leaf baskets, etc.) from the following circumstance, related by himself.—"I used," said he, "to go out of the town [Er-Rei] and sit by a river on the banks of which was abundance of palm-leaves; and it occurred to my mind to make every day five baskets [ḳuffehs], and to throw them into the river, for my amusement, as if I were obliged to do so. My time was so passed for many days: at length, one day, I thought I would walk after the baskets, and see whither they had gone: so I proceeded awhile along the bank of the river, and found an old woman sitting sorrowful. On that day I had made nothing. I said to her, 'Wherefore do I see thee sorrowful?' She answered, 'I am a widow: my husband died leaving five daughters, and nothing to maintain them; and it is my custom to repair every day to this river, and there come to me, upon the surface of the water, five baskets, which I sell, and by means of them I procure food; but to-day they have not come, and I know not what to do.' Upon hearing this, I raised my head

[1] Mir-át ez-Zemán, events of the year 291.

towards heaven, and said, 'O my God, had I known that I had more than five children to maintain, I had laboured more diligently.'" He then took the old woman to his house, and gave her money and flour, and said to her, "Whenever thou wantest anything, come hither and take what may suffice thee."[1]

An irresistible influence has often been exercised over the minds of princes and other great men by reputed saints. Many a Muslim Monarch has thus been incited (as the Kings of Christendom were by Peter the Hermit) to undertake religious wars, or urged to acts of piety and charity, or restrained from tyranny, by threats of Divine vengeance to be called down upon his head by the imprecations of a welee. 'Alee, the favourite son of the Khaleefeh El-Ma-moon, was induced for the sake of religion to flee from the splendour and luxuries of his father's court, and after the example of a self-denying devotee to follow the occupation of a porter in a state of the most abject poverty at El-Baṣrah, fasting all the day, remaining without sleep at night in a mosque, and walking barefooted, until, under an accumulation of severe sufferings, he prematurely ended his days, dying on a mat. The honours which he refused to receive in life were paid to him after his death: his rank being discovered by a ring and paper which he left, his corpse was anointed with camphor and musk and aloes, wrapped

[1] Mirát ez-Zemán, l. l.

in fine linen of Egypt, and so conveyed to his distressed father at Baghdád.[1]

Self-denial I have before mentioned as one of the most important means by which to attain the dignity of a welee. A very famous saint, Esh-Shiblee, is said to have received from his father an inheritance of sixty millions of deenárs (a sum incredible, and probably a mistake for sixty thousand, or for sixty million dirhems) besides landed property, and to have expended it all in charity: also, to have thrown into the Tigris seventy hundred-weight of books, written by his own hand during a period of twenty years.[2]

Sháh El-Karmánee, another celebrated saint, had a beautiful daughter, whom the Sulṭán of his country sought in marriage. The holy man required three days to consider his sovereign's proposal, and in the mean time visited several mosques, in one of which he saw a young man humbly occupied in prayer. Having waited till he had finished, he accosted him, saying, "My son, hast thou a wife?" Being answered "No," he said, "I have a maiden, a virtuous devotee, who hath learned the whole of the Ḳur-án, and is amply endowed with beauty. Dost thou desire her?"—"Who," said the young man, "will marry me to such a one as thou hast described, when I possess no more than three dirhems?"—"*I* will marry thee to

[1] Mirát-ez-Zemán, events of the year 218.

[2] Ibid., events of the year 334.

her," answered the saint: "she is my daughter, and I am Sháh the son of Shujáạ El-Karmánee: give me the dirhems that thou hast, that I may buy a dirhem's worth of bread, and a dirhem's worth of something savoury, and a dirhem's worth of perfume." The marriage-contract was performed; but when the bride came to the young man, she saw a stale cake of bread placed upon the top of his mug; upon which she put on her izár, and went out. Her husband said, "Now I perceive that the daughter of Sháh El-Karmánee is displeased with my poverty." She answered, "I did not withdraw from fear of poverty, but on account of the weakness of thy faith, seeing how thou layest by a cake of bread for the morrow." [1]

One of my friends in Cairo, Abu-l-Ḳásim of Jeelán, entertained me with a long relation of the mortifications and other means which he employed to attain the rank of a welee. These were chiefly self-denial and a perfect reliance upon Providence. He left his home in a state of voluntary destitution and complete nudity, to travel through Persia and the surrounding countries and yet more distant regions if necessary, in search of a spiritual guide. For many days he avoided the habitations of men, fasting from daybreak till sunset, and then eating nothing but a little grass or a few leaves or wild fruits, till by degrees he habituated himself to almost total abstinence from

[1] Es-Suyooṭee's Nuzhet el-Mutaämmil, section 4.

every kind of nourishment. His feet, at first blistered and cut by sharp stones, soon became callous; and in proportion to his reduction of food, his frame, contrary to the common course of nature, became (according to his own account) more stout and lusty. Bronzed by the sun, and with his black hair hanging over his shoulders (for he had abjured the use of the razor), he presented in his nudity a wild and frightful appearance, and on his first approaching a town, was surrounded and pelted by a crowd of boys; he therefore retreated, and, after the example of our first parents, made himself a partial covering of leaves; and this he always afterwards did on similar occasions, never remaining long enough in a town for his leafy apron to wither. The abodes of mankind he always passed at a distance, excepting when several days' fast, while traversing an arid desert, compelled him to obtain a morsel of bread or a cup of water from the hand of some charitable fellow-creature.

One thing that he particularly dreaded was to receive relief from a sinful man, or from a demon in the human form. In passing over a parched and desolate tract, where for three days he had found nothing to eat, not even a blade of grass, nor a spring from which to refresh his tongue, he became overpowered with thirst, and prayed that God would send him a messenger with a pitcher of water. "But," said he, "let the water be in a green Baghdádee pitcher, that I may know it to be from Thee, and not from the Devil; and when I ask the bearer to give me to drink, let him pour it over my head, that I may not too much gratify my carnal desire."—"I looked behind me," he continued, "and saw a man bearing a green Baghdádee pitcher of water, and said to him, 'Give me to drink;' and he came up to me, and poured the contents over my head, and departed! By Allah it was so!"

Rejoicing in this miracle, as a proof of his having attained to a degree of wiláyeh (or saintship), and refreshed by the water, he continued his way over the desert, more firm than ever in his course of self-denial, which, though imperfectly followed, had been the means of his being thus distinguished. But the burning thirst returned shortly after, and he felt himself at the point of sinking under it, when he beheld before him a high hill, with a rivulet running by its base. To the summit of this hill he determined to ascend, by way of mortification, before he would taste the water, and this point, with much difficulty, he reached at the close of day. Here standing, he saw approaching, below, a troop of horsemen, who paused at the foot of the hill, when their chief, who was foremost, called out to him by name, "O Abu-l-Ḳásim! O Jeelánee! Come down and drink!"—but persuaded by this that he was Iblees with a troop of his sons, the evil Genii, he withstood the temptation, and remained stationary until the deceiver with his attendants had passed on and were out of sight. The sun had then set; his thirst had somewhat abated; and he only drank a few drops.

Continuing his wanderings in the desert, he found upon a pebbly plain an old man with a long white beard, who accosted him, asking of what he was in search. "I am seeking," he answered, "a spiritual guide; and my heart tells me that thou art the guide I seek." "My son," said the old man, "thou seest yonder a saint's tomb; it is a place where prayer is answered; go thither, enter it, and seat thyself: neither eat nor drink nor sleep; but occupy thyself solely, day and night, in repeating silently, 'Lá iláha illa-lláh' (There is no deity but God); and let not any living creature see thy lips move in doing so; for among the peculiar virtues of these words is this, that they may be uttered without any motion of the lips. Go, and peace be on thee!"

"Accordingly," said my friend, "I went thither. It was a small square building, crowned by a cupola; and the door was open. I entered, and seated myself, facing the niche and the oblong monument over the grave. It was evening, and I commenced my silent professions of the unity, as directed by my guide; and at dusk I saw a white figure seated beside me, as if assisting in my devotional task. I stretched forth my hand to touch it; but found that it was not a material substance; yet there it was: I saw it distinctly. Encouraged by this vision, I continued my task for three nights and days without intermission, neither eating nor drinking, yet increasing in strength both of body and of spirit; and on the third day, I saw written upon the whitewashed walls of the tomb and on the ground, and in the air, wherever I turned my eyes, 'Lá iláha illa-lláh;' and whenever a fly entered the tomb, it formed these words in its flight. By Allah it was so! My object was now fully attained: I felt myself endowed with supernatural knowledge: thoughts of my friends and acquaintances troubled me not; but I knew where each one of them was, in Persia, India, Arabia, and Turkey, and what each was doing. I experienced an indescribable happiness. This state lasted several years; but at length I was insensibly enticed back to worldly objects: I came to this country; my fame as a calligraphist drew me into the service of the government; and now see what I am, decked with pelisses and shawls, and with this thing [a diamond order] on my breast; too old, I fear, to undergo again the self-denial necessary to restore me to true happiness, though I have almost resolved to make the attempt."

Soon after this conversation, he was deprived of his office, and died of the plague. He was well known to have passed several years as a wandering devotee; and his sufferings, combined with enthusiasm, perhaps disordered his imagination, and made him believe that he really saw the strange sights which he described to me; for there was an appearance of earnestness and sincerity in his manner, such as I thought could hardly be assumed by a conscious impostor.

Insanity, however, if not of a very violent and dangerous nature, is commonly regarded by Muslims as a quality that entitles the subject of it to be esteemed as a saint; being supposed to be the abstraction of the mind from worldly affairs, and its total devotion to God. This popular superstition is a fertile source of imposture; for, a reputation for sanctity being so easily obtained and supported, there are numbers of persons who lay claim to it from motives of indolence and licentiousness, eager to receive alms merely for performing the tricks of madmen, and greedy of indulging in pleasures forbidden by the law; such indulgences not being considered in their case as transgressions by the common people, but rather as indications of holy frenzy. From my own observation I should say that lunatics or idiots, or impostors, constitute the majority of the persons reputed to be saints among the Muslims of the present day; and most of those who are not more than slightly tinged with insanity are darweeshes.

A reputed saint of this description in Cairo, in whom persons of some education put great faith, affected to have a particular regard for me. He several times accosted me in an abrupt manner, acquainted me with the state of my family in England, and uttered incoherent predictions respecting me, all of which communications, excepting one which he qualified with an "in sháa-lláh" (or "if it be the will of God"), I must confess, proved to be true; but I must also state that he was acquainted with two of my friends who might have materially assisted him to frame these predictions, though they protested to me that they had not done so. The following extract from a journal which I kept in Cairo during my last visit to Egypt, will convey some idea of this person, who will serve as a picture of many of his fraternity. —To-day (Nov. 6th, 1834), as I was sitting in the shop of the Pásha's booksellers, a reputed saint, whom I have often seen here, came and seated himself by me, and began, in a series of abrupt sentences, to relate to me various matters respecting me, past, present, and to come. He is called the sheykh 'Alee el-Leythee. He is a poor man, supported by alms; tall and thin and very dark, about thirty years of age, and wears nothing at present but a blue shirt and a girdle and a padded red cap. "O Efendee," he said, "thou hast been very anxious for some days. There is a grain of anxiety remaining in thee yet. Do not fear. There is a letter coming to thee by sea, that will bring thee good news." He then proceeded to tell me of the state of my family, and that all were well excepting one, whom he particularized by description, and who he stated to be then suffering from an intermittent fever. [This proved to be exactly true.] "This affliction," he continued, "may be removed by prayer; and the excellences of the next night, the night of [*i.e.* preceding] the first Friday of the month of Rejeb, of Rejeb, the holy Rejeb, are very great. I wanted to ask thee for something to-day; but I feared, I feared greatly. Thou must be invested with the wiláyeh [*i.e.* be made a welee]: the welees love thee, and the Prophet loves thee. Thou must go to the sheykh Musṭafà El-Munádee and the sheykh El-Bahácc.[1] Thou must be a welee." He then took my right hand, in the manner commonly practised in the ceremony which admits a person a darweesh, and repeated the Fátiḥah; after which he added, "I have admitted thee my darweesh." Having next told me of several circumstances relating to my family—matters of an unusual nature—with singular minuteness and truth, he added, "To-night, if it be the will of God, thou shalt see the Prophet in thy sleep, and El-Khiḍr and the Seyyid El-Bedawee. This is Rejeb, and I wanted to ask thee—but I feared—I wanted to ask of thee four piasters, to buy meat and bread and oil and radishes. Rejeb! Rejeb! I have great offices to do for thee to-night."

Less than a shilling for all he promised was little

[1] These are two very celebrated welees.

enough: I gave it him for the trouble he had taken; and he uttered many abrupt prayers for me. In the following night, however, I saw in my sleep neither Moḥammad, nor El-Khiḍr, nor the Seyyid El-Bedawee, unless, like Nebuchadnezzar, I was unable on awaking to remember my dreams.

Some reputed saints of the more respectable class, to avoid public notice, wear the general dress and manners of their fellow-countrymen, and betray no love of ostentation in their acts of piety and self-denial; or live as hermits in desert places, depending solely upon Providence for their support, and are objects of pious and charitable visits from the inhabitants of near and distant places, and from casual travellers. Others distinguish themselves by the habit of a darweesh, or by other peculiarities, such as a long and loose coat (called dilḳ) composed of patches of cloth of various colours, long strings of beads hung upon the neck, a ragged turban, and a staff with shreds of cloth of different colours attached to the top; or obtain a reputation for miraculous powers by eating glass, fire, serpents, etc. Some of those who are insane, and of those who feign to be so, go about, even in crowded cities, in a state of perfect nudity, and are allowed to commit with impunity acts of brutal sensuality which the law, when appealed to, should punish with death. Such practices are forbidden by the religion and law even in the cases of saints; but common and deeply-rooted superstition prevents their punishment.

During the occupation of Egypt by the French, the Commander-in-chief, Menou, applied to the sheykhs (or 'Ulamà) of the city for their opinion "respecting those persons who were accustomed to go about in the streets in a state of nudity, crying out and screaming, and arrogating to themselves the dignity of wiláyeh, relied upon as saints by the generality of the people, neither performing the prayers of the Muslims nor fasting," asking whether such conduct was permitted by the religion, or contrary to the law. He was answered, "Conduct of this description is forbidden, and repugnant to our religion and law and to our traditions." The French General thanked them for this answer, and gave orders to prevent such practices in future, and to seize every one seen thus offending; if insane, to confine him in the Máristán (or hospital and lunatic asylum); and if not insane, to compel him either to relinquish his disgusting habits, or to leave the city.[1]

Of reputed saints of this kind, thus writes an enlightened poet, El-Bedree El-Ḥijázee :—

"Would that I had not lived to see every fool esteemed among men as a Ḳuṭb!
Their learned men take him as a patron, nay, even as Lord, in place of the Possessor of Heaven's throne.

---

[1] El-Jabartee's History, vol. iii., events of the month of Shaạbán, 1215 (A.D. 1800-1801).

Forgetting God, they say, 'Such a one from all mankind can remove affliction.'
When he dies, they make for him a place of visitation, and strangers and Arabs hurry thither in crowds:
Some of them kiss his tomb, and some kiss the threshold of the door, and the very dust.
Thus do the idolaters act towards their images, hoping so to obtain their favour."

These lines are quoted by El-Jabartee, in his account of a very celebrated modern saint, the seyyid 'Alee El-Bekree (events of Rabeeạ eth-Thánee, 1214). A brief history of this person will not be here misplaced, as it will present a good illustration of the general character and actions of those insane individuals who are commonly regarded as saints.

The seyyid 'Alee El-Bekree was a mejzoob (or insane person) who was considered an eminent welee, and much trusted in: for several years he used to walk naked about the streets of Cairo, with a shaven face, bearing a long nebboot (or staff), and uttering confused language, which the people attentively listened to, and interpreted according to their desires and the exigencies of their states. He was a tall, spare man, and sometimes wore a shirt and a cotton skull-cap; but he was generally barefooted and naked. The respect with which he was treated induced a woman, who was called the sheykhah Ammooneh, to imitate his example further than decency allowed: she followed him whithersoever he went, covered at first with her izár (or large cotton veil thrown over the head and body), and muttering, like him, confused language. Entering private houses with him, she used to ascend to the ḥareems, and gained the faith of the women, who presented her with money and clothes, and spread abroad that the sheykh 'Alee had looked upon her, and affected her with religious frenzy, so that she had become a weleeyeh, or female saint. Afterwards, becoming more insane and intoxicated, she uncovered her face, and put on the clothing of a man; and thus attired she still accompanied the sheykh, and the two wandered about, followed by numbers of children and common vagabonds; some of whom also stripped off their clothes in imitation of the sheykh, and followed, dancing; their mad actions being attributed (like those of the woman) to religious frenzy, induced by his look or touch, which converted them into saints The vulgar and young, who daily followed them, consequently increased in numbers; and some of them, in passing through the market-streets, snatched away goods from the shops, thus exciting great commotion wherever they went. When the sheykh sat down in any place, the crowd stopped, and the people pressed to see him and his mad companions. On these occasions the woman used to moụnt upon the maṣṭabah of a shop, or ascend a hillock, and utter disgusting language, sometimes in Arabic, and sometimes in Turkish, while many persons among her audience would kiss her hands to derive a blessing. After having persevered for some time in this course, none preventing them, the party entered one day the lane leading from the principal street of the city to the house of the Ḳáḍee, and were seized by a Turkish officer there residing, named Jaạfar Káshif, who, having brought them into his house, gave the sheykh some food, and drove out the spectators, retaining the woman and the mejzoobs, whom he placed in confinement. He then liberated the sheykh 'Alee, brought out the woman and the mejzoobs and beat them, sent the woman to the Máristán and there confined her, and set at large the rest, after they had prayed for mercy and clothed themselves and recovered from their intoxication. The woman remained awhile confined in the Máristán, and when liberated lived alone as a sheykhah, believed in by men and women, and honoured as a saint with visits and festivals.

The seyyid 'Alee, after he had thus been deprived of his companions and imitators, was constrained to lead a different kind of life. He had a cunning brother, who, to turn the folly of this saint to a good account, and fill his own purse, (seeing how great faith the people placed in him, as the Egyptians are prone to do in such a case,) confined him in his house, and clothed him, asserting that he had his permission to do so, and that he had been invested with the dignity of Ḳuṭb. Thus he contrived to attract crowds of persons, men and women, to visit him. He forbade him to shave his beard, which consequently grew to its full size; and his body became fat and stout from abundance of food and rest; for, while he went about naked, he was, as before mentioned, of a lean figure. During that period he used generally to pass the night wandering without food through the streets in winter and summer. Having now servants to wait upon him, whether sleeping or waking, he passed his time in idleness, uttering confused and incoherent words, and sometimes laughing and sometimes scolding; and in the course of his idle loquacity he could not but let fall some words applicable to the affairs of some of his listening visitors, who attributed such expressions to his supernatural knowledge of the thoughts of their hearts, and interpreted them as warnings or prophecies. Men and women, and particularly the wives of the grandees, flocked to him with presents and votive offerings, which enriched the coffers of his brother; and the honours which he received ceased not with his death. His funeral was attended by multitudes from every quarter. His brother buried him in the mosque of Esh-Sharáïbee, in the quarter of the Ezbekeeyeh, made for him a maḳṣoorah (or railed enclosure) and an oblong monument over the grave, and frequently repaired thither with readers of the Ḳur-án, munshids to sing odes in his honour, flag-bearers, and other persons, who wailed and screamed, rubbed their faces against the bars of the window before his grave, and caught the air of the place in their hands to thrust it into their bosoms and pockets. Men and women came crowding together to visit his tomb, bringing votive offerings and wax candles and eatables of various kinds to distribute for his sake to the poor.[1] The oblong monument over his grave, resembling a large chest, was covered, when I was in Cairo, with a black stuff ornamented by a line of words from the Ḳur-án, in white characters, surrounding it. A servant who accompanied me during my rides and walks used often to stop as we passed this tomb, and touch the wooden bars of the window above mentioned with his right hand, which he then kissed to obtain a blessing.

In most cases greater honour is paid to a reputed saint after his death, than he receives in his life. A small, square, whitewashed building, crowned with a dome, is generally erected as his tomb, surrounding an oblong monument of stone, brick, or wood, which is immediately over the sepulchral vault. At least one such building forms a conspicuous object close by, or within, almost every Arab village; for the different villages, and different quarters of every town and city, have their respective patron saints, whose tombs are frequently visited, and are the scenes of periodical

[1] El-Jabartee's History, vol. ii., obituary of the year 1207, and events of Rejeb, 1200; and vol. iii., events of Rabeeạ eth-Thánee, 1214.

festivals, generally celebrated once in every year. The tombs of many very eminent saints are mosques; and some of these are large and handsome edifices, the monument being under a large and lofty dome and surrounded by an enclosure of wooden railings, or of elegantly worked bronze. In these buildings also, and in some others, the monument is covered with silk or cotton stuff ornamented with words from the Ḳur-án, which form a band around it. Many buildings of the more simple kind erected in honour of saints, and some of the larger description, are mere cenotaphs, or cover only some relic of the person to whom they are dedicated. The tombs and cenotaphs, or shrines of saints, are visited by numerous persons, and on frequent occasions; most commonly on a particular day of the week. The object of the visitor, in general, is to perform some meritorious act, such as taking bread, or other food, or money, for the poor, or distributing water to the thirsty, on account of the saint, to increase his rewards in heaven, and at the same time to draw down a blessing on himself; or to perform a sacrifice of a sheep, goat, calf, or other animal, which he has vowed to offer, if blessed with some specific object of desire, or to obtain general blessings; or to implore the saints' intercession in some case of need. The flesh of the devoted animal is given to the poor. The visitors also often take with them palm-branches, or sprigs of myrtle, or roses or other flowers, to lay upon the monument, as they do when they visit the tombs of their relations. The visitor walks round the monument, or its enclosure, from left to right, or with his left side towards it (as the pilgrims do round the Kaạbeh), sometimes pausing to touch its four angles or corners with his right hand, which he then kisses; and recites the opening chapter of the Ḳur-án (the Fátiḥah) standing before one or each of its four sides. Some visitors repeat also the chapter of Yá-Seen (the 36th,) or employ a person to recite this, or even the whole of the Ḳur-án, for hire. The reciter afterwards declares that he transfers the merit of this work to the soul of the deceased saint. Any private petition the visitor offers up on his own account, imploring a favourable answer for the sake of the saint, or through his intercession; holding his hands before his face like an open book, and then drawing them down his face. Many a visitor, on entering the tomb, kisses the threshold, or touches it with his right hand, which he then kisses; and on passing by it, persons often touch the window and kiss the hand thus honoured.

The great periodical or annual festivals are observed with additional ceremonies, and by crowds of visitors. These are called Moolids (more properly Mólids), and are held on the anniversary of the birth of the saint or in commemoration of that event. Persons are then hired to recite the Ḳur-án in and near the tomb during the day; and others, chiefly darweeshes, employ themselves during the night in performing zikrs, which consist in repeating the name of God, or the profession of his unity, etc., in chorus, accompanying the words by certain motions of the head, hands, or whole body; munshids, at intervals, singing religious odes or love songs during these performances, to the accompaniment of a náy, which is a kind of flute, or the arghool, which is a double reed-pipe. These moolids are scenes of rejoicing and of traffic, which men and boys and girls attend to eat sweetmeats, and drink coffee and sherbets, or to amuse themselves with swinging, or turning on a whirligig, or witnessing the feats of conjurers, or the performances of dancers; and to which tradesmen repair to sell or barter their goods. The visitors to the great moolids of the Seyyid Aḥmad El-Bedawee at Ṭanṭà in the Delta of Egypt, which are great fairs as well as religious festivals, are almost as numerous as the pilgrims at Mekkeh. During a moolid, the inhabitants of the houses in the neighbourhood of the tomb hang lamps before their houses, and spend a great part of the night listening to the story-tellers at the coffee-shops, or attending the zikrs.

These latter performances, though so common among the Arabs, are inconsistent with the spirit of the Mohammadan religion, and especially with respect to music, which was not employed in religious ceremonies until after the second century of the Flight.

The Imám Aboo-Bekr Eṭ-Ṭoosee, being asked whether it were lawful or not to be present with people who assembled in a certain place and read a portion of the Ḳur-án, and, after a munshid had recited some poetry, would dance and become excited and play upon tambourines and pipes,—answered, that such practices were vain, ignorant, and erroneous, not ordained by the Ḳur-án or the Traditions of the Prophet, but invented by those Israelites who worshipped the Golden Calf; that the Prophet and his companions used to sit so quietly that a bird might alight upon the head of any one of them and not be disturbed; that it was incumbent on the Sulṭán and his vicegerents to prevent such persons from entering the mosques and other places for these purposes; and that no one who believed in God and the Last Day should be present with them or assist them in their vain performances: such, he asserted, was the opinion of the Imáms of the Muslims.[1] Some eminent doctors, however, have contended for the lawfulness of these practices.

The following is an account of a Zikr I myself witnessed. The zikkeers (or performers of the zikr), who were about thirty in number, sat cross-legged upon matting extended close to the houses on one side of the street, in the form of an oblong ring.[2] Within

[1] El-Isḥáḳee, reign of El-Mutawekkil. Cp. De Sacy, Chrest. Arabe, i. 122, 123 (2nd ed.).

[2] The zikr here described was performed near the tomb of a saint,

this ring, along the middle of the matting, were placed three very large wax candles, each about four feet high, and stuck in a low candlestick. Most of the zikkeers were Aḥmedee darweeshes, persons of the lower orders, and meanly dressed: many of them wore green turbans. At one end of the ring were four munshids (or singers of religious odes), and with them was a player on the kind of flute called náy. I procured a small seat of palm-sticks from a coffee-shop close by, and, by means of a little pushing and the assistance of my servant, obtained a place with the munshids, and sat there to hear a complete act, or "mejlis," of the zikr; which act commenced at about three o'clock, Muslim time (or three hours after sunset), and continued two hours.

The performers began by reciting the opening chapter of the Ḳur-án, all together, their sheykh, or chief, first exclaiming, "El-Fátiḥah!" They then chanted the following words:—"O God, bless our lord Moḥammad among the former generations; and bless our lord Moḥammad among the latter generations; and bless our lord Moḥammad in every time and period; and bless our lord Moḥammad in the highest degree, unto the day of judgment; and bless all the prophets and apostles among the inhabitants of the

for whose sake it was celebrated. The ceremony is often performed in a sepulchral mosque, and often in the court, or in a chamber, of a private house.

heavens and of the earth; and may God (whose name be blessed and exalted!) be well pleased with our lords and our masters, those persons of illustrious estimation, Aboo-Bekr and 'Omar and 'Othmán and 'Alee, and with all the favourites of God. God is our sufficiency; and excellent is the Guardian! There is no strength nor power but in God, the High, the Great! O God! O our Lord! O thou liberal of pardon! O thou most bountiful of the most bountiful! O God! Amen!"—They were then silent for three or four minutes; and again recited the Fátiḥah, but silently. This form of prefacing the zikr is commonly used by almost all orders of darweeshes in Egypt.

The performers now began the zikr itself. Sitting in the manner above described, they chanted, in slow measure, "Lá iláha illa-lláh" ("There is no deity but God") to the following air:—

Lá i - lá - ha il - la-l - láh. Lá i - lá - ha i - l - la - l -
D.C.
- lá - h. Lá i - lá - ha il- la-l - láh.

bowing the head and body twice in each repetition of "Lá iláha illa-lláh." Thus they continued about a quarter of an hour; and then, for about the same space of time, they repeated the same words to the same air, but in a quicker measure and with correspondingly quicker motions. In the mean time, the munshids frequently sang to the same (or a variation of the same) air portions of a ḳaṣeedeh or of a muweshshaḥ;[1] an ode of a similar nature to the Song of Solomon, generally alluding to the Prophet as the object of love and praise; and at frequent intervals one of them sang out the word "meded," implying an invocation for spiritual or supernatural aid.

The zikkeers, after having performed as above described, next repeated the same words to a different air for about the same length of time; first very slowly, then quickly. The air was as follows:—

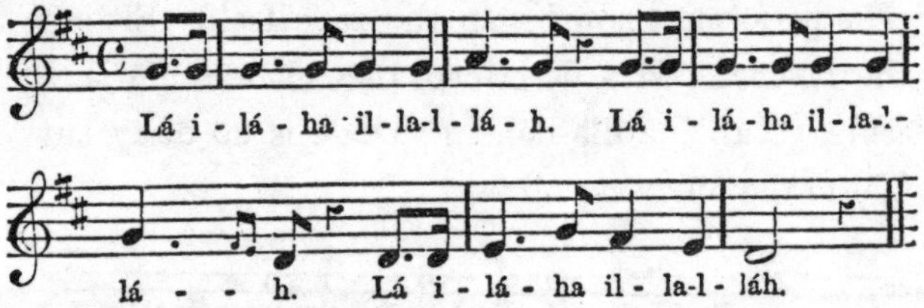
Lá i - lá - ha il - la-l - lá - h. Lá i - lá - ha il - la-l -
lá - - h. Lá i - lá - ha il - la-l - láh.

Then they repeated these words again, to the following air, in the same manner:

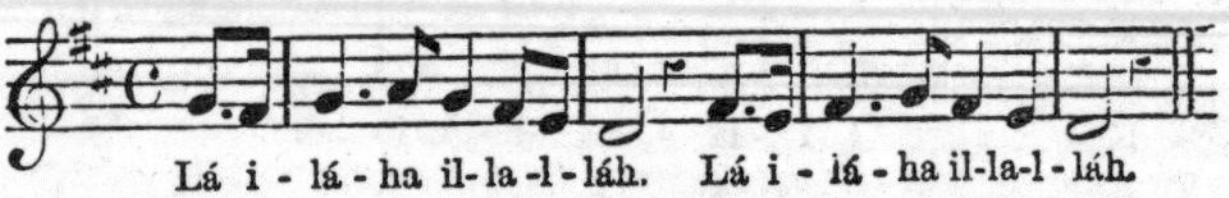
Lá i - lá - ha il- la -l - láh. Lá i - lá - ha il-la-l - láh.

They next rose, and, standing in the same order in which they had been sitting, repeated the same words

[1] For an example, see Modern Egyptians, ch. xxiv.

to another air. After which, still standing, they repeated these words in a very deep and hoarse tone, laying the principal emphasis upon the word "Lá" and the penultimate syllable of the following words, and uttering apparently with a considerable effort: the sound much resembled that which is produced by beating the rim of a tambourine. Each zikkee turned his head alternately to the right and left at each repetition of "Lá iláha illa-lláh." One of them, a eunuch, at this part of the zikr, was seized with an epileptic fit, evidently the result of a high state of religious excitement; but nobody seemed surprised at it, for occurrences of this kind at zikrs are not uncommon. All the performers now seemed much excited; repeating their ejaculations with greater rapidity, violently turning their heads, and sinking the whole body at the same time: some of them jumping. The eunuch above mentioned was again seized with fits several times; and I generally remarked that this happened after one of the munshids had sung a line or two and exerted himself more than usual to excite his hearers: the singing was, indeed, to my taste, very pleasing. The contrast presented by the vehement and distressing exertions of the performers at the close of the zikr, and their calm gravity and solemnity of manner at the commencement, was particularly striking. Money was collected during the performance for the munshids. The zikkeers receive no pay.

The most approved and common mode of entertaining guests at modern private festivities among the Arabs is by a Khatmeh, which is the recitation of the whole of the Ḳur-án. Three or more persons of the inferior class of the professors of religion and law, who are called faḳeehs (vulgarly, fiḳees) are usually hired for this purpose. Schoolmasters, and students of the collegiate mosques who devote themselves to religion and law, are the persons most commonly thus employed. Their mode of recitation is a peculiar kind of chanting, which, when well executed, I found very agreeable, at least for an hour or so: but the guests seldom have to listen to the chanting of the whole of the Ḳur-án: the reciters usually accomplish the greater portion of their task, in a somewhat hurried manner, before the guests have assembled, each of them chanting in turn a certain portion, as a thirtieth part of the whole (called a juz), or half of one of these sections (a ḥezb), or, more commonly, a quarter (rubạ). Afterwards they chant more leisurely, and in a more musical manner; but still by turns. These recitations of the whole of the Ḳur-án are performed on various festive occasions, but are most usual after a death; the merit of the performance being transferred to the soul of the deceased.

In the year 1834, when I was residing in Cairo, a General in the service of Moḥammad 'Alee hired a large party of men to perform a recital of the Ḳur-án in his house in that city, and then went up into his ḥareem and strangled his wife, in consequence of a report which accused her of inchastity. The religious ceremony was designed as preparatory to this act, though the punishment of the woman was contrary to the law, since her husband neither produced four witnesses of the imputed crime, nor allowed her to clear herself of the charge by her own oath. Another case of diligence in the performance of a religious duty, accompanied by the contemplation of murder, but murder on a larger scale, occurred in the same city shortly after. Suleymán Agha, the Siláḥdár, being occupied in directing the building of a public fountain as a work of charity to place to the account of a deceased brother, desired to extend the original plan of the structure; and to do this, it was necessary that he should purchase two houses adjoining the plot in which the foundations had been laid: but the owners of these houses refused to sell them, and he therefore employed a number of workmen to undermine them by night and cause them to fall upon their inhabitants. His scheme, however, but partially succeeded, and no lives were sacrificed. This man was notorious for cruelty, but he was a person of pleasing and venerable countenance and engaging manners: whenever I chanced to meet him, I received from him a most gracious salutation. He died before I quitted Egypt.

CHAPTER IV.

MAGIC.

An implicit belief in magic is entertained by almost all Muslims; and him among them who denies its truth they regard as a freethinker or an infidel. Some are of opinion that it ceased on the mission of Moḥammad; but these are comparatively few. Many of the most learned Muslims, to the present age, have deeply studied it; and a much greater number of persons of inferior education (particularly schoolmasters) have more or less devoted their time and talents to the pursuit of this knowledge. Recourse is had to it for the discovery of hidden treasures, for alchymical purposes, for the acquisition of the knowledge of futurity, to procure offspring, to obtain the affection of a beloved object, to effect cures, to guard against the influence of the evil eye, to afflict or kill an enemy or a rival, and to attain various other objects of desire.

There are two descriptions of magic: one is spiritual, and regarded by all but freethinkers as true;

the other, natural, and denounced by the more religious and enlightened as deceptive.

I. Spiritual magic, which is termed er-Rooḥánee (vulg. Rowḥánee), chiefly depends upon the virtues of certain names of God and passages from the Ḳur-án, and the agency of Angels and Jinn. It is of two kinds: High and Low ('Ilwee and Suflee), or Divine and Satanic (Raḥmánee, *i.e.* relating to "the Compassionate," and Sheyṭánee).

1. Divine magic is regarded as a sublime science, and is studied only by good men, and practised only for good purposes. Perfection in this branch of magic consists in the knowledge of "the most great name" of God (el-Ism el-Aạẓam); but this knowledge is imparted to none but the peculiar favourites of heaven. By virtue of this name, which was engraved on his seal-ring, Suleymán (Solomon) subjected to his dominion the Jinn and the birds and the winds. By pronouncing it, his minister Áṣaf, also, transported in an instant to the presence of his sovereign in Jerusalem the throne of the Queen of Sheba.[1] But this was a small miracle to effect by such means; for by uttering this name a man may even raise the dead. Other names of the Deity, commonly known, are believed to have particular efficacies when uttered or written; as also are the names of the Prophet; and Angels and good Jinn are said to be rendered subservient to the purposes

[1] Ḳur. xxvii. 40; and Commentary of the Jeláleyn.

of divine magic by means of certain invocations. Of such names and invocations, together with words unintelligible to the uninitiated in this science, passages from the Ḳur-án, mysterious combinations of numbers, and peculiar diagrams and figures, are chiefly composed written charms employed for good purposes. Enchantment, when used for benevolent purposes, is regarded by the vulgar as a branch of lawful or divine magic; but not so by the learned: and the same remark applies to the science of divination.

2. Satanic magic, as its name implies, is a science depending on the agency of the Devil and the inferior evil Jinn, whose services are obtained by means similar to those which propitiate, or render subservient, the good Jinn. It is condemned by the Prophet and all good Muslims, and only practised for bad purposes.

Bábil, or Babel, is regarded by the Muslims as the fountain head of the science of magic, which was, and, as most think, still is, taught there to mankind by two fallen angels, named Hároot and Mároot, who are there suspended by the feet in a great pit closed by a mass of rock. According to the account of them generally received as correct, these two angels, in consequence of their want of compassion for the frailties of mankind, were rendered, by God, susceptible of human passions, and sent down upon the earth to be tempted. They both sinned, and being permitted to choose whether they would be punished in this life or in the other, chose the former. But they were sent down not merely to experience temptation, being also appointed to tempt others by means of their knowledge of magic; though it appears that they were commanded not to teach this art to any man "until they had said, 'Verily we are a temptation; therefore be not an unbeliever.'"[1] The celebrated traditionist, Mujáhid, is related to have visited them under the guidance of a Jew. Having removed the mass of rock from the mouth of the pit or well, they entered. Mujáhid had been previously charged by the Jew not to mention the name of God in their presence; but when he beheld them, resembling in size two huge mountains, and suspended upside-down, with irons attached to their necks and knees, he could not refrain from uttering the forbidden name; whereupon the two angels became so violently agitated that they almost broke the irons which confined them, and Mujáhid and his guide fled back in consternation.[2]

Enchantment, which is termed es-Seḥr, is almost universally acknowledged to be a branch of satanic magic; but some few persons assert that it *may* be, and by some *has* been, studied with good intentions, and practised by the aid of good Jinn: consequently, that there is such a science as *good* enchantment,

[1] Ḳur. ii. 96.

[2] El-Ḳazweenee, account of the well of Bábil, in his 'Ajaïb el-Makhlooḳát.

which is to be regarded as a branch of *divine* or *lawful* magic. The metamorphoses are said to be generally effected by means of spells or invocations to the Jinn, accompanied by the sprinkling of water or dust, etc., on the object to be transformed. Persons are said to be enchanted in various ways: some, paralyzed, or even deprived of life; others, affected with irresistible passion for certain objects; others, again, rendered demoniacs; and some, transformed into brutes, birds, etc. The evil eye is believed to enchant in a very powerful and distressing manner. This was acknowledged even by the Prophet.[1] Diseases and death are often attributed to its influence. Amulets,[2] which are mostly written charms, of the kind above described, are worn by many Muslims with the view of counteracting, or preserving from, enchantment; and for the same purpose, many ridiculous ceremonies are practised.

Divination, which is termed el-Kiháneh, is pronounced on the highest authority to be a branch of

[1] See Mishkát el-Maṣábeeḥ, ii. 374.

[2] "Talisman," is a corruption of the Arabic word "ṭalsam." I write this latter word in accordance with the manner in which it is generally pronounced by the Arabs, and the manner in which my sheykh has written it; by some it is written "ṭilsem," and "ṭilism." It is a term applied to mystical characters; and also to seals, images, etc., upon which such characters are engraved or inscribed. These characters are astrological, or of some other magical kind. The purposes for which ṭalsams are contrived are various; one has the property of preserving from enchantment, or from a particular accident, or a variety of evils; another protects a treasure with which it is deposited; a third, by being rubbed, procures the presence and services of a Jinnee.

satanic magic, though not believed to be so by all Muslims. According to an assertion of the Prophet what a fortune-teller says may sometimes be true; because one of the Jinn steals away the truth, and carries it to the magician's ear: for the Angels come down to the region next the earth (the lowest heaven), and mention the works that have been pre-ordained in heaven; and the Devils (or evil Jinn) listen to what the Angels say, and hear the orders predestined in heaven and carry them to the fortune-tellers. It is on such occasions that shooting-stars are hurled at the Devils.[1] It is said that "the diviner obtains the services of the Sheyṭán by magic arts, and by names [invoked], and by the burning of perfumes, and he informs him of secret things: for the Devils, before the mission of the Apostle of God," it is added, "used to ascend to heaven and hear words by stealth."[2] That the evil Jinn are believed still to ascend sufficiently near to the lowest heaven to hear the conversation of the Angels, and so to assist magicians, appears from the former quotation, and is asserted by all Muslims. The discovery of hidden treasures before alluded to, is one of the objects for which divination is most studied. The mode of divination called Ḍarb el-Mendel is by some supposed to be effected by the aid of evil Jinn; but the more en-

[1] See Mishkát el-Maṣábeeḥ, ii. 384 ff.; and above, 33 and 38.

[2] Account of the early Arabs, in the Mir-át ez-Zemán.

lightened of the Muslims regard it as a branch of natural magic.[1]

There are certain modes of divination which cannot properly be classed under the head of spiritual magic, but require a place between the account of this science and that of natural magic. The most important of these branches of Kiháneh is Astrology, which is called 'Ilm en-Nujoom. This is studied by many Muslims in the present day; and its professors are often employed by the Arabs to determine a fortunate period for laying the foundation of a building, commencing a journey, etc.; but more frequently by the Persians and Turks. The Prophet pronounced astrology to be a branch of magic.[2] Another branch of Kiháneh is Geomancy, called Ḍarb er-Raml;[3] a mode of divination from certain marks made on sand (whence its appellation), or on paper; and said to be chiefly founded on astrology. The science called ez-Zijr, or el-'Eyáfeh, is a third branch of Kiháneh; being

[1] Some curious performances of this kind, by means of a fluid mirror of ink, have been described in my "Account of the Manners and Customs of the Modern Egyptians," ch. xii., and in No. 117 of the *Quarterly Review*.

[2] Mishkát el-Maṣábeeḥ, ii. 385.

[3] Or Ḍarb er-Ramal, also called 'Ilm er-Raml. There are several treatises on Geomancy by Eastern writers: but I have not met with any of these; nor have I seen a geomantic tablet. I have only seen the mode of performing geomantic experiments upon paper. The invention of the science is ascribed by some to Idrees (Enoch), by some to Daniel, by some to Ham the son of Noah, and by others to Hermes Trismegistus.

divination or auguration chiefly from the motions and positions or postures of birds or of gazelles and other beasts of the chase. Thus what was termed a Sániḥ, that is, such an animal standing or passing with its right side towards the spectator, was esteemed among the Arabs as of good omen; and a Báriḥ, or an animal of this kind with its left side towards the spectator, was held as inauspicious.[1] El-Ḳiyáfeh, under which term are included Chiromancy and its kindred sciences, is a fourth branch of Kiháneh. Et-Tefául, or the taking an omen, particularly a good one, from a name or words accidentally heard or seen or chosen from a book, belongs to the same science.

The taking a fál, or omen, from the Ḳur-án is generally held to be lawful. Various trifling events are considered as ominous. For instance, a Sulṭán quitting his palace with his troops, a standard happened to strike a "thureiyà" (a cluster of lamps, so called from resembling the Pleiades), and broke them: he drew from this an evil omen, and would have relinquished the expedition; but one of his chief officers said to him, "O our Lord, thy standards have reached the Pleiades;"—and, being relieved by this remark, he proceeded, and returned victorious.[2] The

[1] Mir-át ez-Zemán, l. l.

[2] El-Isḥáḳee, in his account of the reign of El-Moʿtaṣim, the son of Hároon.

interpretation of dreams, termed Taạbeer el-Menámát, must also be classed among the branches of this science. According to the Prophet, it is the only branch of divination worthy of dependance. "Good dreams," said he, "are one of the parts of prophecy," and "nothing else of prophecy remains." "Good dreams are from God; and false dreams from the Devil." "When any one of you has a bad dream, spit three times over your left shoulder, and seek protection with God from the Devil thrice; and turn from the side on which the dream was, to the other."[1] This rule is observed by many Muslims. Dreams are generally so fully relied upon by them as to be sometimes the means of deciding contested points in history and science. The sight, in a dream, of anything green or white, or of water, is considered auspicious; anything black or red, or fire, inauspicious.

This firm belief in dreams will be well illustrated by the following anecdote, which was related to me in Cairo, shortly after the terrible plague of the year 1835, by the sheykh Moḥammad Eṭ-Ṭanṭáwee, who had taken the trouble of investigating the fact, and had ascertained its truth.

A tradesman, living in the quarter of El-Ḥanafee, in Cairo, dreamed during that plague that eleven persons were carried out from his house to be buried, victims of this disease. He awoke in a state of the

[1] Mishkát el-Maṣábeeḥ, ii. 388.

greatest distress and alarm, reflecting that eleven was the total number of the inhabitants of his house, including himself, and that it would be vain in him to attempt, by adding one or more members to his household, to elude the decree of God and give himself a chance of escape: so calling together his neighbours, he informed them of his dream, and was counselled to submit with resignation to a fate so plainly foreshown, and to be thankful to God for the timely notice with which he had been mercifully favoured. On the following day, one of his children died; a day or two after, a wife; and the pestilence continued its ravages among his family until he remained in his house alone. It was impossible for him now to entertain the slightest doubt of the entire accomplishment of the warning: immediately, therefore, after the last death that had taken place among his household, he repaired to a friend at a neighbouring shop, and calling to him several other persons from the adjoining and opposite shops, he reminded them of his dream, acquainted them with its almost complete fulfilment, and expressed his conviction that he, the eleventh, should very soon die. "Perhaps," said he, "I shall die this next night: I beg of you, therefore, for the sake of God, to come to my house early to-morrow morning, and the next morning and the next if necessary, to see if I be dead, and, when dead, that I am properly buried; for I have no one with me to wash and shroud me. Fail not to do me this service, which will procure you a recompense in heaven. I have bought my grave-linen: you will find it in a corner of the room in which I sleep. If you find the door of the house latched, and I do not answer to your knocking, break it open."

Soon after sunset he laid himself in his lonely bed, though without any expectation of closing his eyes in sleep; for his mind was absorbed in reflections upon the awful entry into another world, and a review of his past life. As the shades of night gathered around him he could almost fancy that he beheld, in one faint object or another in his gloomy chamber, the dreadful person of the Angel of Death: and at length he actually perceived a figure gliding in at the door, and approaching his bed. Starting up in horror, he exclaimed, "Who art thou?"—and a stern and solemn voice answered, "Be silent! I am 'Azraeel, the Angel of Death!"—"Alas!" cried the terrified man; "I testify that there is no deity but God, and I testify that Moḥammad is God's Apostle! There is no strength nor power but in God, the High, the Great! To God we belong, and to Him we must return!"—He then covered himself over with his quilt, as if for protection, and lay with throbbing heart, expecting every moment to have his soul torn from him by the inexorable messenger. But moments passed away, and minutes, and hours, yet without his experiencing any hope of escape; for he imagined that the Angel was waiting for him to resign himself, or had left him for a while, and was occupied in receiving first the souls of the many hundred human beings who had attained their predestined term in that same night and in the same city, and the souls of the thousands who were doomed to employ him elsewhere.

Daybreak arrived before his sufferings terminated; and his neighbours, coming according to their promise, entered his chamber, and found him still in bed; but observing that he was covered up and motionless as a corpse, they doubted whether he were still alive, and called to him. He answered, with a faint voice, "I am not yet dead; but the Angel of Death came to me in the dusk of the evening, and I expect him every moment to make his return, to take my soul: therefore trouble me not; but see me washed and buried."—"But why," said his friends, "was the street-door left unlatched?"—"I latched it," he answered, "but the Angel of Death may have opened it."—"And who," they asked, "is the man in the court?" He answered, "I know of no man in the court: perhaps the Angel who is waiting for my soul has made himself visible to you, and been mistaken in the twilight for a man."—"He is a thief," they said, "who has gathered together everything in the house that he could carry away, and has been struck by the plague while doing so, and now lies dead in the court, at the foot of the stairs, grasping in his hand a silver candlestick."—The master of the house, after hearing this, paused for a moment, and then, throwing off his quilt, exclaimed, "Praise be to God, the Lord of all creatures! That is the eleventh, and I am safe! No doubt it was that rascal who came to me and said that he was the Angel of Death. Praise be to God! Praise be to God!"

This man survived the plague, and took pleasure in relating the above story. The thief had overheard his conversation with his neighbours, and, coming to his house in the dusk, had put his shoulder to the wooden lock, and so raised the door and displaced the latch within. There is nothing wonderful in the dream, nor in its accomplishment; the plague of 1835 entirely desolated many houses, and was mostly fatal to the young; and all the inhabitants of the house in question were young excepting the master.

The distinction of fortunate and unfortunate days should also here be mentioned. Thursday and Friday, especially the latter, are considered fortunate; Monday and Wednesday, doubtful; Sunday, Tuesday, and Saturday, especially the last, unfortunate. It is said that there are seven evil days in every [lunar] month: namely, the third, on which Ḳábeel (Cain) killed Hábeel (Abel); the fifth, on which God cast down Adam from paradise, and afflicted the people of Yoonus (Jonas), and on which Yoosuf (Joseph) was cast into the well; the thirteenth, on which God took away the wealth of Eiyoob (Job), and afflicted him, and took away the kingdom from Suleymán (Solomon), and on which the Jews killed the prophets; the sixteenth, on which God exterminated and buried the people of Looṭ (Lot), and transformed three hundred Christians into swine and Jews into apes, and on which the Jews sawed asunder Zekeriyà (Zacharịah); the twenty-first, on which Pharaoh was born, and on which he was drowned, and on which his nation was afflicted with the plagues; the twenty-fourth, on which Numrood (Nimrod) killed seventy women, and cast El-Khaleel (Abraham) into the fire, and on which was slaughtered the camel of Ṣáliḥ; and the twenty-fifth, on which the suffocating wind was sent upon the people of Hood.[1]

II. Natural magic, which is called es-Seemiyà, is regarded by most persons of the more enlightened classes of Muslims as altogether a deceptive art, no more worthy of respect than legerdemain; but it seems to be nearly allied to enchantment, for it is said to effect, in appearance, the most wonderful transformations, and to cause the most extraordinary visions; affecting the senses and imagination in a manner similar to opium. This and other drugs are supposed by some persons to be the chief means by which such illusions are caused; and perfumes, which are generally

[1] El-Isḥáḳee, close of his account of the reign of El-Emeen.

burnt in these performances, may operate in a similar manner. As such things are employed in performances of the kind called Ḍarb el-Mendel, before mentioned, these feats are regarded by many as effected by natural magic, notwithstanding what has been said above respecting the services of evil Jinn being procured by means of perfumes. Alchymy (El-Keemiyà) is a branch of natural magic. It is studied by many Muslims of the present day, and by some of considerable talents and attainments.

The most celebrated of the magicians who have gained notoriety in Egypt during the course of the last hundred years was the sheykh Aḥmad Ṣádoomeh, who flourished somewhat more than sixty years ago.[1] Several persons of Cairo, men of intelligence and of good education, have related to me various most marvellous stories of his performances, on the authority of eye-witnesses whom they considered veracious; but a more credible account of this magician I have found in the work of the excellent historian of Modern Egypt. This author mentions the sheykh Ṣádoomeh as an aged man of venerable appearance who derived his origin from the town of Semennood in the Delta, and who acquired a very great and extensive celebrity for his attainments in spiritual and natural magic, and for holding converse, face to face, with Jinn, and causing them to appear to other persons, even to the blind, as

[1] I write in 1837.

men acquainted with him informed the historian. His contemporaries, says this writer, entertained various opinions respecting him; but, among them, a famous grammarian and general scholar, the sheykh Ḥasan El-Kafráwee, regarded him as a first-rate saint, who performed evident miracles; this learned man pronouncing as such the effects of "his legerdemain and natural magic." His fame he describes as having increased until he was induced to try an unlucky experiment.

A Memlook chief, Yoosuf Bey, saw some magic characters written on the body of one of his female slaves, and, exasperated by jealousy, commanded her with a threat of instant death to tell him who had done this. She confessed that a woman had taken her to the sheykh Ṣádoomeh, and that he had written this charm to attract to her the Bey's love. Upon hearing this, he instantly sent some attendants to seize the magician, put him to death, and throw him into the Nile; which was done.[1] But the manner in which the seizure was made, as related to me by one of my friends, deserves to be mentioned. Several persons, one after another, endeavoured to lay hold upon him; but every arm that was stretched forth for this purpose was instantly paralyzed, through a

[1] El-Jabartee's History, account of the death of Yoosuf Bey in the year of the Flight 1191; and account of the death of the Sheykh Ḥasan El-Kafráwee in the year 1202.

spell muttered by the magician; until a man behind him thrust a gag into his mouth, and so stopped his enchantments.

Of the stories related to me of Ṣádoomeh's miracles, the following will serve as a specimen:—In order to give one of his friends a treat, he took him to the distance of about half an hour's walk into the desert on the north of Cairo; here they both sat down, upon the pebbly and sandy plain, and, the magician having uttered a spell, they suddenly found themselves in the midst of a garden, like one of the gardens of paradise, abounding with flowers and fruit-trees of every kind, springing up from a soil clothed with verdure brilliant as the emerald and irrigated by numerous streamlets of the clearest water. A repast of the most delicious viands and fruits and wines was spread before them by invisible hands; and they both ate to satiety, taking copious draughts of the various wines. At length, the magician's guest sank into a deep sleep; and when he awoke, he found himself again in the pebbly and sandy plain, with Ṣádoomeh still by his side.

The reader will probably attribute this vision to a dose of opium or some similar drug; and such I suppose to have been the means employed; for I cannot doubt the integrity of the narrator, though he would not admit such an explanation,—regarding the whole as an affair of magic effected by the operation of the Jinn.

CHAPTER V.

COSMOGRAPHY.

WHEN we call to mind how far the Arabs surpassed their great master, Aristotle, in natural and experimental philosophy, and remember that their brilliant discoveries constituted an important link between those of the illustrious Greek and of our scarcely less illustrious countryman, Roger Bacon, their popular system of cosmography becomes an interesting subject for our consideration.

According to the common opinion of the Arabs (an opinion sanctioned by the Ḳur-án, and by assertions of their Prophet, which almost all Muslims take in their literal sense), there are Seven Heavens, one above another, and Seven Earths, one beneath another; the earth which we inhabit being the highest of the latter, and next below the lowest heaven.[1] The upper surface

[1] This notion of the seven heavens appears to have been taken from the "seven spheres;" the first of which is that of the Moon; the second, of Mercury; the third, of Venus; the fourth, of the Sun; the fifth, of Mars; the sixth, of Jupiter; and the seventh, of Saturn; each of which orbs was supposed to revolve round the earth in its proper sphere. So also the idea of the seven earths seems to have been

of each heaven and of each earth are believed to be nearly plane, and are generally supposed to be circular; and are said to be five hundred years' journey in width. This is also said to be the measure of the depth or thickness of each heaven and each earth, and of the distance between each heaven or earth and that next above or below it. Thus is explained a passage of the Ḳur-án in which it is said that God hath created seven heavens and as many earths, or stories of the earth, in accordance with traditions from the Prophet.[1]

Traditions differ respecting the fabric of the seven heavens. In the most credible account, according to a celebrated historian, the first is described as formed of emerald; the second, of white silver; the third, of large white pearls; the fourth, of ruby; the fifth, of red gold; the sixth, of yellow jacinth; and the seventh, of shining light.[2]

Some assert Paradise to be in the seventh heaven; and, indeed, I have found this to be the general opinion of my Muslim friends: but the author above quoted proceeds to describe, next above the seventh heaven, seven seas of light; then, an undefined

taken from the division of the earth into seven climates; a division which has been adopted by several Arab geographers.

[1] Ḳur. lxv. 12, and Moḥammad's answers to 'Abd-Allah Ibn-Selám, quoted by Ibn-El-Wardee (MS.); and Mekḥool, quoted by the same author; and Mishkát el-Maṣábeeḥ, ii. 652, 653.

[2] Ibn-Esh-Shiḥneh (MS.).

number of veils, or separations, of different substances, seven of each kind; and then, Paradise, which consists of seven stages, one above another; the first (Dár el-Jelál, or the Mansion of Glory), of white pearls; the second (Dár es-Selám, or the Mansion of Peace), of ruby; the third (Jennet el-Ma-wà, or the Garden of Rest), of green chrysolite; the fourth (Jennet en-Khuld, or the Garden of Eternity), of green[1] coral; the fifth (Jennet en-Na'eem, or the Garden of Delight), of white silver; the sixth (Jennet el-Firdós, or the Garden of Paradise), of red gold; and the seventh (Jennet 'Adn, or the Garden of Perpetual Abode, or of Eden), of large pearls; this last overlooking all the former, and canopied by the Throne of the Compassionate ('Arsh Er-Raḥmán). These several regions of Paradise are described in some traditions as forming so many degrees, or stages, ascended by steps.

Though the opinion before mentioned respecting the form of the earth which we inhabit is that generally maintained by the Arabs, there have been, and still are, many philosophical men among this people who have argued that it is a globe, because, as El-Ḳazweenee says, an eclipse of the moon has been observed to happen at different hours of the night in eastern and western countries. Thus we find Ptolemy's measurement of the earth quoted and explained by Ibn-El-Wardee:—The circumference of the earth is

[1] In another MS. of the same author, "yellow."

24,000 miles, or 8,000 leagues, the league being three miles; the mile, 3,000 royal cubits; the cubit, three spans; the span, twelve digits; the digit, five barley-corns placed side by side; and the width of the barley-corn, six mule's-hairs. El-Maḳreezee [† 1442] also, among the more intelligent Arabs, describes[1] the globular form of the earth, and its arctic and antarctic regions, with their day of six months, and night of six months, and their frozen waters, etc.

For ourselves, however, it is necessary that we retain in our minds the opinions first stated, with regard to the form and dimensions of our earth; agreeing with those Muslims who allow not philosophy to trench upon revelation or sacred traditions. It is written, say they, that God hath "spread out the earth,"[2] "as a bed,"[3] and "as a carpet;"[4] and what is round or globular cannot be said to be spread out, nor compared to a bed, or a carpet. It is therefore decided to be an almost plane expanse. The continents and islands of the earth are believed by the Arabs (as they were by the Greeks in the age of Homer and Hesiod) to be surrounded by "the Circumambient Ocean," el-Baḥr el-Moḥeeṭ; and this ocean is described as bounded by a chain of mountains called Ḳáf, which encircle the whole as a ring, and

---

[1] In his Khiṭaṭ (MS.).
[2] Ḳur. xiii. 3, and several other places.
[3] Ḳur. ii. 20, and lxxviii. 6.
[4] Ḳur. lxxi. 18.

confine and strengthen the entire fabric. With respect to the extent of the earth, our faith must at least admit the assertion of the Prophet, that its width (as well as its depth or thickness) is equal to five hundred years' journey, allotting the space of two hundred to the sea, two hundred to uninhabited desert, eighty to the country of Yájooj and Májooj (Gog and Magog), and the rest to the remaining creatures:[1] nay, vast as these limits are, we must rather extend than contract them, unless we suppose some of the heroes of the "Thousand and One Nights" to travel by circuitous routes. Another tradition will suit us better, wherein it is said, that the inhabited portion of the earth is, with respect to the rest, as a tent in the midst of a desert.[2]

But even according to the former assertion it will be remarked that the countries now commonly known to the Arabs (from the western extremity of Africa to the eastern limits of India, and from the southern confines of Abyssinia to those of Russia,) occupy a comparatively insignificant portion of this expanse. They are situated in the middle; Mekkeh, according to some, —or Jerusalem, according to others,—being exactly in the centre. Adjacent to the tract occupied by these countries are other lands and seas, partially known to the Arabs. On the north-west, with respect to the

[1] Mekḥool, quoted by Ibn-El-Wardee.

[2] Wahb Ibn-Munebbih, quoted by El-Maḳreezee in his Khiṭaṭ.

central point, lies the country of the Christians or Franks, comprising the principal European nations; on the north, the country of Yájooj and Májooj, before mentioned, occupying, in the maps of the Arabs, large tracts of Asia and Europe; on the north-east, central Asia; on the east, Eṣ-Ṣeen (China); on the south-east, the sea or seas of El-Hind (India), and Ez-Zinj (Southern Ethiopia), the waves of which (or of the former of which) mingle with those of the sea of Eṣ-Ṣeen, beyond; on the south, the country of the Zinj; on the south-west, the country of the Soodán, or Blacks; on the west is a portion of the Circumambient Ocean, which surrounds all the countries and seas already mentioned, as well as immense unknown regions adjoining the former, and innumerable islands interspersed in the latter.

These *terrae incognitae* are the scenes of some of the greatest wonders described in the "Thousand and One Nights;" and are mostly peopled with Jinn (Genii.) On the Moḥeeṭ, or Circumambient Ocean, is the 'Arsh Iblees, or Throne of Iblees: in a map accompanying my copy of the work of Ibn-El-Wardee, a large yellow tract is marked with this name, adjoining Southern Africa. The western portion of the Moḥeeṭ is often called "the Sea of Darkness" (Baḥr eẓ-Ẓulumát, or, Baḥr eẓ-Ẓulmeh). Under this name (and the synonymous appellation of el-Baḥr el-Muzlim) the Atlantic Ocean is described by the author just mentioned; though, in the introduction to his work, he says that the Sea of Darkness surrounds the Moḥeeṭ. The former may be considered either as the western or the more remote portion of the latter.

In the dark regions (Eẓ-Ẓulumát, from which, perhaps, the above-mentioned portion of the Moḥeeṭ takes its name),[1] in the south-west quarter of the earth, according to the same author, is the Fountain of Life, of which El-Khiḍr[2] drank, and by virtue of which he still lives and will live till the day of judgment. This mysterious person, whom the vulgar and some others regard as a prophet and identify with Ilyás (Elias, Elijah), and whom some confound with St. George, was, according to the more approved opinion of the learned, a just man or saint, the Wezeer and counsellor of the first Dhu-l-Ḳarneyn, who was a universal conqueror, but an equally doubtful personage, contemporary with the patriarch Ibráheem (Abraham). El-Khiḍr is said to appear frequently to Muslims in perplexity, and to be generally clad in green garments; whence, according to some, his name (which signifies "green"). The Prophet Ilyás is also related to have drunk of the Fountain of Life. During the day-time, it is said, El-Khiḍr wanders upon the seas, and directs voyagers who go astray; while Ilyás perambulates the moun-

[1] Ibn-El-Wardee, however, says that its name is derived from its terrors and difficulties.

[2] [Cp. Lane's Selections from the Ḳur-án, 128 ff., 2nd ed. 1879.]

tains or deserts, and directs persons who chance to be led astray by the Ghools: but at night they meet together, and guard the rampart of Yájooj and Májooj,[1] to prevent these people from making irruptions upon their neighbours. Both, however, are generally believed by the modern Muslims to assist pious persons in distress in various circumstances, whether travelling by land or by water.

The Mountains of Ḳáf, which bound the Circumambient Ocean and form a circular barrier round the whole of our earth, are described by interpreters of the Ḳur-án as composed of green chrysolite, like the green tint of the sky.[2] It is the colour of these mountains, said the Prophet, that imparts a greenish hue to the sky. It is said, in a tradition, that beyond these mountains are other countries; one of gold, seventy of silver, and seven of musk, all inhabited by angels, and each country ten thousand years' journey in length, and the same in breadth.[3] Some say that beyond it are creatures unknown to any but God:[4] but the general opinion is, that the mountains of Ḳáf terminate our earth, and that no one knows what is beyond them. They are the chief abode of the Jinn, or Genii.

It has already been said that our earth is the first,

[1] History of El-Khiḍr in the Mir-át ez-Zemán.

[2] El-Ḳazweenee.

[3] Moḥammad's answers to 'Abd-Allah Ibn-Selám, quoted by Ibn-El-Wardee.

[4] El-Ḳazweenee.

or highest, of seven earths, which are all of equal width and thickness and at equal distances apart. Each of these earths has occupants. The occupants of the first are men, genii, brutes, etc.; the second is occupied by the suffocating wind that destroyed the infidel tribe of Ad; the third, by the stones of Jahennem (or Hell), mentioned in the Ḳur-án in these words, "the fuel of which is men and stones;"[1] the fourth, by the sulphur of Jahennem; the fifth, by its serpents; the sixth, by its scorpions, in colour and size like black mules and with tails like spears; the seventh, by Iblees and his troops.[2]

Whether these several earths are believed to be connected with each other by any means, and if so how, we are not expressly informed; but, that they are supposed to be so is evident. With respect to our earth in particular, as some think, it is said that it is supported by a rock, with which the Mountains of Ḳáf communicate by means of veins or roots; and that when God desires to effect an earthquake at a certain place, He commands the mountain (or rock) to agitate the vein that is connected with that place.[3] But there is another account, describing our earth as upheld by certain successive supports

[1] Ḳur. ii. 22, and lxvi. 6. [2] Mir-át ez-Zemán.

[3] Tradition from the Prophet, recorded by Ibn-'Abbás, and quoted by Ibn-El-Wardee; and by El-Isḥáḳee, in describing an earthquake that happened in his lifetime. See also the next note.

of inconceivable magnitude, which are under the seventh earth; leaving us to infer that the seven earths are in some manner connected together. This account, as inserted in the work of one of the writers above quoted, is as follows:—The earth [under which appellation are here understood the seven earths] was, it is said, originally unstable; "therefore God created an angel of immense size and of the utmost strength, and ordered him to go beneath it [*i.e.* beneath the lowest earth] and place it on his shoulders; and his hands extended beyond the east and west, and grasped the extremities of the earth [or, as related in Ibn-El-Wardee, the seven earths] and held it [or them]. But there was no support for his feet: so God created a rock of ruby, in which were seven thousand perforations, and from each of these perforations issued a sea, the size of which none knoweth but God, whose name be exalted; then he ordered this rock to stand under the feet of the angel. But there was no support for the rock: wherefore God created a huge bull, with four thousand eyes and the same number of ears, noses, mouths, tongues, and feet; between every two of which was a distance of five hundred years' journey; and God, whose name be exalted, ordered this bull to go beneath the rock; and he bore it on his back and his horns. The name of this bull is Kuyootà.[1] But

[1] In Ibn-Esh-Shiḥneh, "Kuyoothán;" the orthography of this word is doubtful, as the vowel-points are not written. As the tradition is related in Ibn-El-Wardee, this bull takes a breath twice in the

there was no support for the bull: therefore God, whose name be exalted, created an enormous fish, that no one could look upon on account of its vast size, and the flashing of its eyes, and their greatness; for it is said that if all the seas were placed in one of its nostrils, they would appear like a grain of mustard-seed in the midst of a desert: and God, whose name be exalted, commanded the fish to be a support to the feet of the bull.[1] The name of this fish is Bahamoot [Behemoth]. He placed, as its support, water; and under the water, darkness: and the knowledge of mankind fails as to what is under the darkness."[2]—Another opinion is, that the [seventh] earth is upon water; the water, upon the rock; the rock, on the back of the bull; the bull, on a bed of sand; the sand, on the fish; the fish, upon a still, suffocating wind; the wind, on a veil of darkness; the darkness, on a mist; and what is beneath the mist is unknown.[3]

It is generally believed that under the lowest earth, and beneath seas of darkness of which the

course of every day (or twenty-four hours): when he exhales, the sea flows; and when he inhales, it ebbs. But it must not be imagined that none of the Arabs has any notion of the true theory of the tides: the more learned among them explain this phenomenon by the influence of the moon. Many of the Arabs attribute earthquakes to the shaking of this bull.

[1] In Ibn-El-Wardee, a quantity of sand is introduced between the bull and the fish.

[2] Ed-Demeeree, on the authority of Wahb Ibn-Munebbih, quoted by El-Isḥáḳee, l. l.

[3] Ibn-El-Wardee.

number is unknown, is Hell, which consists of seven stages, one beneath another. The first of these, according to the general opinion, is destined for the reception of wicked Mohammadans; the second, for the Christians; the third, for the Jews; the fourth, for the Sabians; the fifth, for the Magians; the sixth, for the Idolaters; the seventh, by general consent, for the Hypocrites. Jahennem is the general name for Hell, and the particular name for its first stage.[1] The situation of Hell has been a subject of dispute; some place it in the seventh earth; and some have doubted whether it be above or below the earth which we inhabit.

At the consummation of all things, God, we are told, will take the whole earth in his [left] hand, and the heavens will be rolled together in his right hand;[2] and the earth will be changed into another earth; and the heavens, [into other heavens];[3] and Hell will be brought nigh to the [tribunal of God].[4]

[1] [The other stages are Laẓà, El-Ḥuṭameh, Sa'eer, Saḳar, Jeheem, and Ḥáwiyeh.]

[2] Ḳur. xxxix. 67. [3] Ḳur. xiv. 49. [4] Ḳur. lxxxix. 24.

CHAPTER VI.

LITERATURE.

PERHAPS there are no people in the world who are such enthusiastic admirers of literature, and so excited by romantic tales, as the Arabs. Eloquence, with them, is lawful magic: it exercises over their minds an irresistible influence. "I swear by God," said their Prophet, "verily abuse of infidels in verse is worse to them than arrows."[1]

In the purest, or Heroic Age of Arabic literature, which was anterior to the triumph of the Mohammadan religion, the conquest which the love of eloquence could achieve over the sanguinary and vindictive feelings of the Arabs was most remarkably exemplified in the annual twenty days' fair of 'Okaḍh.

The fair of 'Okáḍh "was not only a great mart opened annually to all the tribes of Arabia; but it was also a literary congress, or rather a general concourse of virtues, of glory and of poetry, whither the

[1] Mishkát el-Maṣábeeḥ, ii. 424. This of course alludes to *Arab* unbelievers. [For a fuller account of ancient Arab poetry, with examples, see my Introduction to Lane's "Selections from the Ḳurán," xiv.–xxxi. 2nd ed. S. L-P.]

hero-poets resorted to celebrate their exploits in rhyming verse, and peacefully to contend for every kind of honour. This fair was held in the district of Mekkeh, between Eṭ-Ṭáïf and Nakhleh and was opened at the new moon of Dhu-l-Ḳaạdeh; that is to say, at the commencement of a period of three sacred months, during which all war was suspended and homicide interdicted. . . . How is it possible to conceive that men whose wounds were always bleeding, who had always acts of vengeance to execute, vengeances to dread, could at a certain epoch impose silence upon their animosities, so as tranquilly to sit beside a mortal enemy? How could the brave who required the blood of a father, a brother, or a son, according to the phraseology of the desert and of the Bible,[1] who long, perhaps, had pursued in vain the murderer,—meet him, accost him peacefully at 'Okaḍh, and only assault with cadences and rhymes him whose presence alone seemed to accuse him of impotence or cowardice,—him whom he was bound to slay, under pain of infamy, after the expiration of the truce? In fine, how could he hear a panegyric celebrating a glory acquired at his own expense, and sustain the fire of a thousand looks, and yet appear unmoved? Had the Arabs no longer any blood in their veins during the continuance of the fair?

"These embarrassing questions . . . were deter-

[1] Genesis ix. 5.

mined [to a great degree], during the age of Arab paganism, in a manner the simplest and most refined: at the fair of 'Okáḍh, the heroes were masked [or veiled]. In the recitations and improvisations, the voice of the orator was aided by that of a rhapsodist or crier, who was stationed near him, and repeated his words. There is a similar office in the public prayers; it is that of the muballigh (transmitter), who is employed to repeat in a loud voice what is said in a lower tone by the Imám. . . . The use of the mask [or veil] might, however, be either adopted or dispensed with *ad libitum;* as is proved by the narratives of a great number of quarrels begun and ended at 'Okáḍh. . . .

"It was in this congress of the Arab poets (and almost every warrior was a poet at the age which I am considering) that the dialects of Arabia became fused into a magic language, the language of the Ḥejáz, which Moḥammad made use of to subvert the world; for the triumph of Moḥammad is nothing else than the triumph of speech."[1] The Ḳur-án is regarded by the Arabs as an everlasting miracle, surpassing all others, appealing to the understanding of every

[1] Lettres sur l'Histoire des Arabes avant l'Islamisme, par Fulgence Fresnel (Paris, 1836, pp. 31 ff.); an author who is at present [1837] devoting talents of the very highest order to the study and illustration of the history and literature of the early Arabs, and to whose conversations and writings I must acknowledge myself indebted for the most valuable information.

generation by its inimitable eloquence. A stronger proof of the power of language over their minds could hardly be adduced; unless it be their being capable of receiving as a credible fact the tradition that both genii and men were attracted by the eloquent reading of David, when he recited the Psalms; that the wild beasts and the birds were alike fascinated; and that sometimes there were borne out from his assembly as many as four hundred corpses of men who died from the excessive delight with which he thus inspired them![1] It may be added, that the recitation or chanting of the Ḳur-án is a favourite means of amusing the guests at modern private festivities.

In what may be termed the Middle Age of Arabic literature, beginning with the triumph of the Mohammadan religion and extending to the foundation of the Empire of Baghdád, the power of eloquence over the educated classes of the Arabs probably increased in proportion as it became less familiar to them: for early in this age they began to simplify their spoken language in consequence of their intercourse with strangers, who could not generally acquire the difficult, old dialect of their conquerors, which consequently began to be confined to literary compositions. That such a change took place at this period appears from several anecdotes interspersed in Arabic works. The Khaleefeh El-Weleed (who reigned

[1] El-Isḥáḳee.

near the close of the first century of the Flight), the son of 'Abd-El-Melik, spoke so corrupt a dialect that he often could not make himself understood by the Arabs of the desert. A ridiculous instance of the mistakes occasioned by his use of the simplified language which is now current is related by Abu-l-Fidà. The same author adds that the father and predecessor of this prince was a man of eloquence, and that he was grieved by the corrupt speech of his son, which he considered as a defect that incapacitated him to be a future ruler of the Arabs, who were still great admirers of purity of speech, though so large a proportion of them spoke a corrupt dialect. So he sent him to a house to be instructed by a grammarian; but after the youth had remained there a long time, he returned to his father more ignorant than before. Vulgarisms, however, would sometimes escape from the mouth of 'Abd-El-Melik himself; yet so sensible was he to eloquence, that when a learned man, with whom he was conversing, elegantly informed him of an error of this kind, he ordered his mouth to be filled with jewels. "These," said his courteous admonisher, "are things to be treasured up, not to be expended:" —and for this delicate hint he was further rewarded with thirty thousand pieces of silver and several costly articles of apparel.[1]

It may be added that this Khaleefeh was in the

[1] El-Isḥáḳee.

beginning of his reign an unjust monarch, but was reclaimed to a sense of his duty by the following means. Being one night unable to sleep, he called for a person to tell him a story for his amusement. " O Prince of the Faithful," said the man thus bidden, "there was an owl in El-Móṣil, and an owl in El-Baṣrah; and the owl of El-Móṣil demanded in marriage for her son the daughter of the owl of El-Baṣrah : but the owl of El-Baṣrah said, 'I will not, unless thou give me as her dowry a hundred desolate farms.' 'That I cannot do,' said the owl of El-Móṣil, 'at present; but if our sovereign (may God, whose name be exalted, preserve him !) live one year, I will give thee what thou desirest.'" This simple fable sufficed to rouse the prince from his apathy, and he thenceforward applied himself to fulfil the duties of his station.[1]

In the most flourishing age of Arabic poetry and general literature and science, beginning with the foundation of the Empire of Baghdád and extending to the conquest of Egypt by the 'Othmánlee Turks, the influence of eloquent and entertaining language upon the character of the Arab sovereigns was particularly exemplified, as the following anecdotes will show.

It is related by El-Aṣma'ee that Hároon Er-Rasheed, at a grand fête which he was giving, ordered the poet Abu-l'Atáhiyeh to depict in verse the volup-

[1] El-Isḥáḳee.

tuous enjoyments of his sovereign. The poet began thus:—

> "Live long in safe enjoyment of thy desires under the shadow of lofty palaces!"

"Well said!" exclaimed Er-Rasheed: "and what next?"

> "May thy wishes be abundantly fulfilled, whether at eventide or in the morning!"

"Well!" again said the Khaleefeh: "then what next?"

> "But when the rattling breath struggles in the dark cavity of the chest,
> Then shalt thou know surely that thou hast been only in the midst of illusions."

Er-Rasheed wept; and Faḍl, the son of Yaḥyà, said, "The Prince of the Faithful sent for thee to divert him, and thou hast plunged him into grief." "Suffer him," said the prince; "for he hath beheld us in blindness, and it displeased him to increase it." [1]

The family of the Barmekees (one of the most brilliant ornaments of which was the Wezeer Jaạfar, who has been rendered familiar to us by the many scenes in which he is introduced in the "Thousand and One Nights") earned a noble and enduring reputation by their attachment to literature and the magnificent rewards they conferred on learned men. It was peculiarly hard, therefore, that literature contributed to their melancholy overthrow. Poets were employed

[1] Fakhr-ed-Deen, in De Sacy, Chrestomathie Arabe.

by their enemies to compose songs artfully pointed against them, to be sung before the prince to whom they owed their power. Of one of these songs, the following lines formed a part:—

> "Would that Hind had fulfilled the promises she made us, and healed the disease under which we suffer!
> That she had once, at least, acted for herself! for imbecile, indeed, is he who doth not so."

"Yea! By Allah! Imbecile!" exclaimed the Khaleefeh, on hearing these verses: his jealousy was roused; and his vengeance soon after fell heavily upon his former favourites.[1]

One of the Khaleefehs having invited the poets of his day to his palace, a Bedawee, carrying a water-jar to fill at the river, followed them, and entered with them. The Khaleefeh, seeing this poor man with the jar on his shoulder, asked him what brought him thither. He returned for answer these words:—

> "Seeing that this company had girded on the saddles
> To repair to thy overflowing river, I came with my jar."

The Khaleefeh, delighted with his answer, gave orders to fill his jar with gold.[2]

It has long been a common custom of Eastern princes to bestow dresses of honour upon men of literature and science, as well as upon their great officers and other servants. These dresses were of different kinds for persons of different classes or professions. The most usual kind was an ample coat. With dresses of this descrip-

[1] Ibn-Khaldoon. [2] Ḥalbet el-Kumeyt (MS.), chap. vii.

tion were often given gold-embroidered turbans, and sometimes to Emeers (or great military officers) neck-rings or collars (called ṭóḳs), some of which were set with jewels, as also bracelets and swords ornamented with precious stones; and to Wezeers, instead of the ṭóḳ, a necklace of jewels.[1]

The following striking record will convey an idea of the magnificence of some of these dresses of honour, or in other words of the liberality of a Muslim prince, and at the same time of the very precarious nature of his favour. A person chancing to look at a register kept by one of the officers of Hároon Er-Rasheed, saw in it the following entry:—"Four hundred thousand pieces of gold, the price of a dress of honour for Jaạfar, the son of Yaḥyà, the Wezeer." A few days after, he saw beneath this written,—"Ten ḳeeráṭs, the price of naphtha and reeds, for burning the body of Jaạfar, the son of Yaḥyà."[2]

Arab princes and other great men have generally been famous for highly respecting and liberally rewarding men of literature and science, and especially poets. El-Ma-moon and many others are well known to us for their patronage of the learned. Er-Rasheed carried his condescension to them so far as to pour the water on the hands of a blind man, Aboo-Mo'áwiyeh,

[1] El-Maḳreezee's Khiṭaṭ, chapter entitled "Khizánet el-Kisawát."

[2] Fakhr-ed-Deen, ubi supra. The ḳeerat of Baghdád was the twentieth part of a deenár or piece of gold.

one of the most learned persons of his time, previously to his eating with him, to show his respect for science.[1] We have already seen how a Khaleefeh ordered the mouth of a learned man to be filled with jewels. To cram the mouth with sugar or sweetmeats for a polite or eloquent speech, or piece of poetry, has been more commonly done; but the usual presents to learned men were, and are, dresses of honour and sums of money. Ibn-'Obeyd El-Bakhteree, an illustrious poet and traditionist who flourished in the reign of El-Musta'een, is said to have received so many presents that after his death there were found, among the property which he left, a hundred complete suits of dress, two hundred shirts, and five hundred turbans.[2] A thousand pieces of gold were often given, and sometimes ten, twenty, or thirty thousand, and even more, for a few verses; nay, for a single couplet.

The prodigality of Arab princes to men of learning may be exemplified by the following anecdote.—Ḥammád, surnamed Er-Ráwiyeh, or the famous reciter, having attached himself to the Khaleefeh El-Weleed, the son of 'Abd-El-Melik, and shown a contrary feeling towards his brother Hishám, fled, on the accession of the latter, to El-Koofeh. While there, a letter arrived from Hishám, commanding his presence at Damascus: it was addressed to the governor, who, being ordered to treat him with honour, gave him

[1] Fakhr-ed-Deen, ubi supra. [2] D'Herbelot, art. "Bokhteri."

a purse containing a thousand pieces of gold, and despatched him with the Khaleefeh's messenger.

On his arrival at Damascus, he was conducted before Hishám, whom he found in a splendid saloon, seated under a pavilion of red silk surmounted by a dome of yellow brocade, attended by two female slaves of beauty unsurpassed, each holding a crystal ewer of wine. His admission during the presence of members of the king's ḥareem was a very unusual and high honour: the mention of the wine will be explained in the next chapter. After Ḥammád had given the salutation[1] and the Khaleefeh had returned it, the latter told him that he had sent for him to ask respecting a couplet of which he could only remember that it ended with the word "ibreeḳ," which

[1] Various different modes of obeisance are practised by the Muslims. Among these, the following are the more common or more remarkable: they differ in the degree of respect that they indicate, nearly in the order in which I shall mention them; the last being the most respectful:—1. Placing the right hand upon the breast.—2. Touching the lips and the forehead or turban (or the forehead or turban only) with the right hand.—3. Doing the same, but slightly inclining the head during that action.—4. The same as the preceding, but inclining the body also.—5. As above, but previously touching the ground with the right hand.—6. Kissing the hand of the person to whom the obeisance is paid.—7. Kissing his sleeve.—8. Kissing the skirt of his clothing.—9. Kissing his feet.—10. Kissing the carpet or ground before him.—The first five modes are often accompanied by the salutation of "Peace be on you:" to which the reply is, "On you be peace and the mercy of God and his blessings." The sixth mode is observed by servants or pupils to masters, by the wife to the husband, and by children to their father and sometimes to the mother. The last mode is seldom observed but to kings; and in Arabian countries it is now very uncommon.

signifies "a ewer." The reciter reflected awhile, and the lines occurred to his mind, and he repeated them. Hishám cried out in delight that the lines were those he meant; drank a cup of wine, and desired one of the female slaves to hand a cup to Ḥammád. She did so; and the draught, he says, deprived him of one-third of his reason. The Khaleefeh desired him to repeat the lines again, and drink a second cup; and Ḥammád was deprived of another third of his reason in the same manner; and said, "O Prince of the Faithful, two-thirds of my reason have departed from me." Hishám laughed, and desired him to ask what he would before the remaining third should have gone; and the reciter said, "One of these two female slaves." The Khaleefeh laughed again, and said, "Nay, but both of them are thine, and all that is upon them and all that they possess, and beside them fifty thousand pieces of gold."—"I kissed the ground before him," says Ḥammád, "and drank a third cup, and was unconscious of what happened after. I did not awake till the close of the night, when I found myself in a handsome house, surrounded by lighted candles, and the two female slaves were putting in order my clothes and other things. So I took possession of the property, and departed, the happiest of the creatures of God."[1]

In the beginning of the year of the Flight 305 (A.D. 917), two ambassadors from the Greek Emperor

[1] Ḥalbet el-Kumeyt, chap. vii.

(Constantine VII., Porphyrogenitus) arrived in Baghdád on a mission to the Khaleefeh El-Muḳtedir, bringing an abundance of costly presents. They were first received by the Wezeer, who, at the audience which he granted to them in his garden palace, displayed a degree of magnificence that had never before been manifested by any of his rank. Pages, memlooks, and soldiers, crowded the avenues and courts of his mansion, the apartments of which were hung with tapestry of the value of thirty thousand deenárs; and the Wezeer himself was surrounded by generals and other officers on his right and left and behind his seat, when the two ambassadors approached him, dazzled by the splendour that surrounded them, to beg for an interview with the Khaleefeh. El-Muḳtedir, having appointed a day on which he would receive them, ordered that the courts and passages and avenues of his palace should be filled with armed men, and that all the apartments should be furnished with the utmost magnificence. A hundred and sixty thousand armed soldiers were arranged in ranks in the approach to the palace; next to these were the pages of the closets and chief eunuchs, clad in silk and with belts set with jewels, in number seven thousand,—four thousand white and three thousand black,—besides seven hundred chamberlains; and beautifully ornamented boats of various kinds were seen floating upon the Tigris hard by.

The two ambassadors passed first by the palace of the chief chamberlain, and, astonished at the splendid ornaments and pages and arms which they there beheld, imagined that this was the palace of the Khaleefeh. But what they had seen here was eclipsed by what they beheld in the latter, where they were amazed by the sight of thirty-eight thousand pieces of tapestry of gold-embroidered silk brocade, and twenty-two thousand magnificent carpets. Here also were two menageries of beasts, by nature wild but tamed by art and eating from the hands of men: among them were a hundred lions, each with its keeper. They then entered the Palace of the Tree, enclosing a pond from which rose the Tree: this had eighteen branches, with artificial leaves of various colours and with birds of gold and silver (or gilt and silvered) of every variety of kind and size perched upon its branches, so constructed that each of them sang. Thence they passed into the garden, in which were furniture and utensils not to be enumerated; in the passages leading to it were suspended ten thousand gilt coats of mail. Being at length conducted before El-Muḳtedir, they found him seated on a couch of ebony inlaid with gold and silver, to the right of which were hung nine necklaces of jewels, and the like to the left, the jewels of which outshone the light of day. The two ambassadors paused at the distance of about a hundred cubits from the Khaleefeh, with the interpreter. Having left the presence, they were conducted through the palace, and were shown splendidly caparisoned elephants, a giraffe, lynxes, and other beasts. They were then clad with robes of honour, and to each of them was brought fifty thousand dirhems, together with dresses and other presents. It is added that the ambassadors approached the palace through a street called "the Street of the Menárehs," in which were a thousand menárehs or minarets. It was at the hour of noon; and as they passed, the muëddins from all these minarets chanted the call to prayer at the same time, so that the earth almost quaked at the sound, and the ambassadors were struck with fear.[1]

The Orientals well understand how to give the most striking effect to the jewels which they display on their dress and ornaments on occasions of state. Sir John Malcolm, describing his reception by the King of Persia, says, "His dress baffled all description. The ground of his robes was white; but he was so covered with jewels of an extraordinary size, and their splendour, from his being seated where the rays of the sun played upon them, was so dazzling, that it was impossible to distinguish the minute parts which combined to give such amazing brilliancy to his whole figure."

A whimsical story is told of a King who denied to

[1] Mir-át er-Zemán, events of 305.

poets those rewards to which usage had almost given them a claim. This King, whose name is not recorded, had the faculty of retaining in his memory an ode after having only once heard it; and he had a memlook who could repeat an ode that he had twice heard, and a female slave who could repeat one that she had heard thrice. Whenever a poet came to compliment him with a panegyrical ode, the King used to promise him that if he found his verses to be his original composition, he would give him a sum of money equal in weight to what they were written upon. The poet, consenting, would recite his ode; and the King would say, "It is not new, for I have known it some years;" and would repeat it as he had heard it. After which he would add, "And this memlook also retains it in his memory;" and would order the memlook to repeat it: which, having heard it twice, from the poet and the king, he would do. The King would then say to the poet, "I have also a female slave who can repeat it;" and on his ordering her to do so, stationed behind the curtains, she would repeat what she had thus thrice heard: so the poet would go away empty-handed. The famous poet, El Aṣma'ee, having heard of this proceeding, and guessing the trick, determined upon outwitting the King; and accordingly composed an ode made up of very difficult words. But this was not his only preparative measure, another will be presently explained, and a third was to assume the dress of a Bedawee, that he might not be known, covering his face, the eyes only excepted, with a lithám (a piece of drapery) in accordance with a custom of Arabs of the desert.

Thus disguised, he went to the palace, and having asked permission, entered, and saluted the King, who said to him, "Whence art thou, O brother of the Arabs, and what dost thou desire?"

The poet answered, "May God increase the power of the King! I am a poet of such a tribe, and have composed an ode in praise of our Lord the Sulṭán."

"O brother of the Arabs," said the King, "hast thou heard of our condition?"

"No," answered the poet; "and what is it, O King of the age?"

"It is," replied the King, "that if the ode be not thine, we give thee no reward; and if it be thine, we give thee the weight in money of what it is written upon."

"How," said El-Aṣma'ee, "should I assume to myself that which belongs to another, and knowing, too, that lying before kings is one of the basest of actions? But I agree to this condition, O our Lord the Sulṭán."

So he repeated his ode. The King, perplexed, and unable to remember any of it, made a sign to the memlook—but he had retained nothing; and called to the female slave, but she also was unable to repeat a word.

"O brother of the Arabs," said he, "thou hast spoken truth, and the ode is thine without doubt; I have never heard it before: produce, therefore, what it is written upon, and we will give thee its weight in money, as we have promised."

"Wilt thou," said the poet, "send one of the attendants to carry it?"

"To carry what?" asked the King; "is it not upon a paper here in thy possession?"

"No, our lord the Sulṭán," replied the poet; "at the time I composed it I could not procure a piece of paper upon which to write it, and could find nothing but a fragment of a marble column left me by my father; so I engraved it upon this, and it lies in the court of the palace."

He had brought it, wrapped up, on the back of a camel. The King, to fulfil his promise, was obliged to exhaust his treasury; and to prevent a repetition of this trick, (of which he afterwards discovered El-Aṣma'ee to have been the author,) in future rewarded the poets according to the usual custom of kings.[1]

In the present declining age of Arabian learning (which may be said to have commenced about the period of the conquest of Egypt by the 'Othmánlees), literary recreations still exert a magical influence upon the Arabs. Compositions of a similar nature to the tales of the "Thousand and One Nights" (though re-

[1] Ḥalbet el-Kumeyt, chap. viii.

garded by the learned as idle stories unworthy of being classed with their literature) enable numbers of professional story-tellers to attract crowds of delighted listeners to the coffee-shops of the East; and now that the original of this work is printed and to be purchased at a moderate price, it will probably soon in a great measure supersede the romances of Aboo-Zeyd, Eẓ-Ẓáhir, and 'Antarah. As a proof of the powerful fascinations with which the tales of the "Thousand and One Nights" affect the mind of a highly enlightened Muslim, it may be mentioned that the latest native historian of Modern Egypt, the sheykh 'Abd-Er-Raḥmán El-Jabartee, so delighted in their perusal that he took the trouble of refining the language of a copy of them which he possessed, expunging or altering whatever was grossly offensive to morality without the somewhat redeeming quality of wit, and adding many facetiæ of his own and of other literati. What has become of this copy I have been unable, though acquainted with several of his friends, to discover.

The letters of Muslims are distinguished by several peculiarities dictated by the rules of politeness. The paper is thick, white, and highly polished: sometimes it is ornamented with flowers of gold; and the edges are always cut straight with scissors. The upper half is generally left blank, and the writing never occupies any portion of the second side. A notion of the usual style of letters may be obtained from several examples in the "Thousand and One Nights." The name of the person to whom the letter is addressed, when the writer is an inferior or an equal, and even in some other cases, commonly occurs in the first sentence, preceded by several titles of honour; and is often written a little above the line to which it appertains; the space beneath it in that line being left blank: sometimes it is written in letters of gold, or red ink. A king writing to a subject, or a great man to a dependant, usually places his name and seal at the head of his letter. The seal is the impression of a signet (generally a ring, worn on the little finger of the right hand), upon which is engraved the name of the person, commonly accompanied by the words "His [*i.e.* God's] servant," or some other words expressive of trust in God and the like. Its impression is considered more valid than the sign-manual, and is indispensable to give authenticity to the letter. It is made by dabbing some ink upon the surface of the signet and pressing this upon the paper: the place which is to be stamped being first moistened by touching the tongue with a finger of the right hand and then gently rubbing the part with that finger. A person writing to a superior or an equal, or even to an inferior to whom he wishes to show respect, signs his name at the bottom of his letter, next the left side or corner, and places the seal immediately to the right of this: but if he particularly desire to testify his humility, he places it beneath his name, or even partly over the lower edge of the paper, which consequently does not receive the whole of the impression. The letter is generally folded twice in the direction of the writing, and enclosed in a cover of paper, upon which is written the address in some such form as this :—"It shall arrive, if it be the will of God, whose name be exalted, at such a place, and be delivered into the hand of our honoured friend, etc., such a one, whom God preserve." Sometimes it is placed in a small bag, or purse, of silk embroidered with gold.

Many persons of the instructed classes, and some others among the Arabs, often take delight and show much ingenuity and quickness of apprehension in conversing and corresponding by means of signs and emblems, or in a conventional, metaphorical language, not understood by the vulgar in general and sometimes not by any excepting the parties engaged in the intercourse. In some cases, when the main metaphor employed is understood, the rest of the conversation becomes easily intelligible, without any previous explanation; and I have occasionally succeeded in carrying on a conversation of this kind, but I have more frequently been unsuccessful in attempting to divine the nature of a topic in which other persons were engaged. One simple mode of secret conversation or correspondence is by substituting certain letters for other letters.

Many of the women are said to be adepts in this art, or science, and to convey messages, declarations of love, and the like, by means of fruits, flowers, and other emblems. The inability of numbers of women in families of the middle classes to write or read, as well as the difficulty or impossibility frequently existing of conveying written letters, may have given rise to such modes of communication. Lady Mary Wortley Montagu, in one of her charming letters from the East, has gratified our curiosity by a Turkish love-letter of this kind.[1] A specimen of one from an Arab with its answer, may be here added:—An Arab lover sent to his mistress a fan, a bunch of flowers, a silk tassel, some sugar-candy, and a piece of a chord of a musical instrument; and she returned for answer a piece of an aloe-plant, three black cumin-seeds, and a piece of a plant used in washing.[2] His communication is thus interpreted. The fan, being called "mirwaḥah," a word derived from a root which has among its meanings that of "going to any place in the evening,"

[1] The art here mentioned was first made known to Europeans by a Frenchman, M. Du Vigneau, in a work entitled "Secrétaire Turc, contenant l'Art d'exprimer ses pensées sans se voir, sans se parler, et sans s'écrire:" Paris, 1688: in-12. Von Hammer has also given an interesting paper on this subject in the "Mines de l'Orient," No. 1: Vienna, 1809. (Note to Marcel's "Contes du Cheykh El-Mohdy," iii. 327, 328: Paris, 1833.)

[2] Called "ghásool el-azrár." In Delile's Flora Ægyptiaca, the name of ghásool is given to the mesembryanthemum nodiflorum, class icosandria, order pentagynia.

signified his wish to pay her an evening visit: the flowers, that the interview should be in her garden: the tassel, being called "shurrábeh," that they should have sharáb[1] (or wine): the sugar-candy, being termed "sukkar nebát," and "nebát" also signifying "we will pass the night," denoted his desire to remain in her company until the morning: and the piece of a chord, that they should be entertained by music. The interpretation of her answer is as follows. The piece of an aloe-plant, which is called "ṣabbárah" (from "ṣabr," which signifies "patience"—because it will live for many months together without water), implied that he must wait: the three black cumin-seeds explained to him that the period of delay should be three nights: and the plant used in washing informed him that she should then have gone to the bath, and would meet him.[2]

A remarkable faculty is displayed by some Arabs for catching the meaning of secret signs employed in written communications to them, such signs being often used in political and other intrigues. The following is a curious instance.—The celebrated poet El-Mutanebbee, having written some verses in dispraise of Káfoor El-Ikhsheedee, the independent Governor of Egypt, was obliged to flee and hide himself in a distant town. Káfoor was informed of his retreat, and

[1] This name is now given to sherbet.

[2] Ḥalbet el-Kumeyt, chap. x.

desired his secretary to write to him a letter promising him pardon and commanding him to return; but told the writer at the same time that when the poet came he would punish him. The secretary was a friend of the poet, and, being obliged to read the letter to the Prince when he had written it, was perplexed how to convey to El-Mutanebbee some indication of the danger that awaited him. He could only venture to do so in the exterior address; and having written this in the usual form, commencing "In sháa-lláh" (If it be the will of God) "this shall arrive," etc., he put a small mark of reduplication over the "n" in the first word, which he thus converted into "Inna," the final vowel being understood. The poet read the letter and was rejoiced to see a promise of pardon; but on looking a second time at the address was surprised to observe the mark of reduplication over the "n." Knowing the writer to be his friend, he immediately suspected a secret meaning, and rightly conceived that the sign conveyed an allusion to a passage in the Ḳur-án commencing with the word "Inna," and this he divined to be the following:—"Verily the magistrates are deliberating concerning thee, to put thee to death."[1] Accordingly, he fled to another town. Some authors add that he wrote a reply conveying by a similar sign to his friend an allusion to another passage in the Ḳur-án:—"We will never enter the country while

[1] Ḳur. xxviii. 19.

they remain therein."[1] It is probable that signs thus employed were used by many persons to convey allusions to certain words; and such may have been the case in the above-mentioned instance: if not, the poet was indeed a wonderful guesser.

It is commonly believed by the Muslims (learned and unlearned) that all kinds of birds and many (if not all) beasts have a language by which they communicate their thoughts to each other; and we are told in the Ḳur-án[2] that Suleymán (Solomon) was taught the language of birds.[3] I thought that I could boast of an accomplishment very rare in Christian countries, in having learned in Egypt somewhat of this language; for instance, that the common cry of the pigeon is "Allah! Allah!" ("God! God!"); that of the ringdove, "Kereem! Towwáb!" ("Bountiful! Propitious!"—an ejaculation addressed to God); that of the common dove, "Waḥḥidoo rabbakumu-llezeẹ khalaḳakum yeghfir-lakum zembakum!" ("Assert the unity of your Lord who created you, that He may forgive you your sin!"): but I afterwards found that several specimens of this language were given by Ez-Zamakhsheree, and had been published in Europe.[4] The cock cries, "Uzkuru-lláha, yá gháfiloon!" ("Commemorate God, O ye negligent!"): the ḳaṭà (a kind of grouse), "Men seket selim!" ("He who is silent is

[1] Ḳur. v. 27.
[2] Ḳur. xxvii. 16.
[3] Manṭiḳ eṭ-ṭeyr.
[4] Alcoranus Marraccii, p. 511.

safe!") The latter, however, would do better if it did itself attend to the maxim it utters; for its cry (which to the uninstructed in the language of birds sounds merely "kaṭa! kaṭa!"—its own name) tells where it is to be found by the sportsman, and thus causes its own destruction.—Hence the proverb, "More veracious than the kaṭa."

An Arab historian mentions a parrot which recited the Soorat Yá-Seen (or 36th chapter of the Ḳur-án), and a raven which recited the Soorat es-Sijdeh (or 32nd chapter) and which, on arriving at the place of prostration (or verse which should be recited with prostration), would perform that action, and say, "My body prostrateth itself to Thee, and my heart confideth in Thee." But these are not the most remarkable cases of the kind. He affirms that there was a parrot in Cairo which recited the Ḳur-án from beginning to end. The Pásha, he says, desiring to try its talent, caused a man to recite a chapter of the Ḳur-án in its presence, and to pass irregularly from one chapter to another, with the view of leading the bird into error; but, instead of this being the result, the parrot corrected him![1]

[1] El-Isḥáḳee; reign of the Khaleefeh El-Musta'een, the son of El-Moataṣim.

CHAPTER VII.

FEASTING AND MERRY-MAKING.

THE Muslim takes a light breakfast after the morning-prayers, and dinner after the noon-prayers; or a single meal instead of these two, before noon. His principal meal is supper, which is taken after the prayers of sunset. A man of rank or wealth, when he has no guest, generally eats alone; his children eat after him, or with his wife or wives. In all his repasts he is moderate with regard to the quantity which he eats, however numerous the dishes.

In the Middle Ages it appears that the dishes were sometimes, I believe generally, placed upon a round embroidered cloth spread on the floor, and sometimes on a tray, which was either laid on the floor or upon a small stand or stool. The last is the mode now always followed in the houses of the higher and middle classes of the Arabs. The table is usually placed upon a round cloth spread in the middle of the floor, or in a corner next two of the deewáns or low seats which generally extend along three sides of the room. It is composed of a large round tray of silver, or tinned copper, or of brass, supported by a stool, commonly about fifteen or sixteen inches high, made of wood and generally inlaid with mother-of-pearl, and ebony or other wood, or tortoise-shell. When there are numerous guests, two or more such tables are prepared. The dishes are of silver or tinned copper, or china. Several of these are placed upon the tray; and around them are disposed some round flat cakes of bread, with spoons of box-wood, ebony, or other material, and usually two or three limes cut in halves, to be squeezed over certain of the dishes. When these preparations have been made, each person who is to partake of the repast receives a napkin; and a servant pours water over his hands. A basin and ewer of either of the metals first mentioned are employed for this purpose; the former has a cover with a receptacle for a piece of soap in its centre, and with numerous perforations through which the water runs during the act of washing, so that it is not seen when the basin is brought from one person to another. It is indispensably requisite to wash at least the right hand before eating with the fingers anything but dry food; and the mouth also is often rinsed, the water being taken up into it from the right hand. The company sit upon the floor, or upon cushions, or some of them on the deewán, either cross-legged or with the right knee raised: [1] they retain the napkins before mentioned,

[1] A pious Muslim generally sits at his meals with the right knee

or a long napkin, sufficient to surround the tray, is placed upon their knees; and each person, before he begins to eat, says, "In the name of God," or "In the name of God, the Compassionate, the Merciful." The master of the house begins first: if he did not so, some persons would suspect that the food was poisoned. The thumb and two fingers of the right hand serve instead of knives and forks; and it is the usual custom for a person to help himself to a portion of the contents of a dish by drawing it towards the edge, or taking it from the edge, with a morsel of bread, which he eats with it: when he takes too large a portion for a single mouthful, he generally places it on his cake of bread. He takes from any dish that pleases him; and sometimes a host hands a delicate morsel with his fingers to one of his guests. It is not allowable to touch food with the left hand (as it is used for unclean purposes), excepting in a few cases when both hands are required to divide a joint.

Among the more common dishes are the following:—lamb or mutton, cut into small pieces, and stewed with various vegetables, and sometimes with peaches, apricots, or jujubes, and sugar; cucumbers or small gourds, or the fruit of the black or white egg-plant, stuffed with rice and minced meat, vine-leaves or pieces of lettuce-leaf or cabbage-leaf, en-

raised, after the example of the Prophet, who adopted this custom in order to avoid too comfortable a posture in eating, as tempting to unnecessary gratification.

closing a similar composition; small morsels of lamb or mutton, roasted on skewers, and called kebáb; fowls simply roasted or boiled, or boned and stuffed with raisins, pistachio-nuts, crumbled bread, and parsley; and various kinds of pastry and other sweets. The repast is frequently opened with soup; and is generally ended with boiled rice, mixed with a little butter and seasoned with salt and pepper; or after this is served, a water-melon or other fruit, or a bowl of a sweet drink composed of water with raisins and sometimes other kinds of fruit boiled in it, and then sugar, with a little rose-water added to it when cool. The meat, having generally little fat, is cooked with clarified butter, and is so thoroughly done that it is easily divided with the fingers.

A whole lamb, stuffed in the same manner as the fowls above mentioned, is not a very uncommon dish; but one more extraordinary, of which 'Abd-El-Laṭeef gives an account[1] as one of the most remarkable that he had seen in Egypt, I am tempted to describe. It was an enormous pie, composed in the following manner:—Thirty pounds of fine flour being kneaded with five pounds and a half of oil of sesame, and divided into two equal portions, one of these was spread upon a round tray of copper about four spans in diameter. Upon this were placed three lambs, stuffed with pounded meat fried with oil of sesame

[1] Hist. Aegypt. Compend. 180–182. (Oxon. 1800.)

and ground pistachio-nuts, and various hot aromatics, such as pepper, ginger, cinnamon, mastic, coriander-seed, cumin-seed, cardamom, nut [or nutmeg?], etc. These were then sprinkled with rose-water infused with musk; and upon the lambs, and in the remaining spaces, were placed twenty fowls, twenty chickens, and fifty smaller birds; some of which were baked, and stuffed with eggs; some, stuffed with meat; and some, fried with the juice of sour grapes, or that of limes, or some similar acid. To the above were added a number of small pies; some filled with meat and others with sugar and sweetmeats; and sometimes the meat of another lamb, cut into small pieces, and some fried cheese. The whole being piled up in the form of a dome, some rose-water infused with musk and aloes-wood was sprinkled upon it; and the other half of the paste first mentioned was spread over, so as to close the whole: it was then baked, wiped with a sponge, and again sprinkled with rose-water infused with musk.

On certain periodical festivals, and on other occasions it has long been, and still is, a custom of Muslim princes to give public feasts to all classes of their subjects, in the palace. El-Maḳreezee quotes a curious account of the feasts which were given on the festival following Ramaḍán to the inhabitants of Cairo by the Fáṭimee Khaleefehs. At the upper end of a large saloon was placed the sereer (or couch) of the monarch, upon which he sat with the Wezeer on his right. Upon this seat was placed a round silver table, with various delicacies, of which they alone ate. Before it, and extending nearly from the seat to the other extremity of the saloon, was set up a kind of table or platform (simáṭ) of painted wood, resembling a number of benches placed together, ten cubits or about eighteen or nineteen feet in width. Along the middle of this were ranged twenty-one enormous dishes, each containing twenty-one baked sheep, three years old and fat, together with fowls, pigeons, and young chickens, in number 350 of each kind, all of which were piled together in an oblong form to the height of the stature of a man, and enclosed with dry sweetmeat. The spaces between these dishes were occupied by nearly five hundred other dishes of earthenware, each of which contained seven fowls, and was filled with sweetmeats of various kinds. The table was strewn with flowers, and cakes of bread made of the finest flour were arranged along each side; there were also two great edifices of sweetmeats, each weighing 17 cwt., which were carried thither by porters with shoulder poles, and one of them was placed at the commencement and the other at the close of this sumptuous banquet. When the Khaleefeh and the Wezeer had taken their seats upon the couch, the officers of state, who were distinguished by neck-rings or collars, and the inferior members of the Court, seated themselves in the order of their respective ranks; and when they had eaten, they gave place to others. Two officers distinguished themselves at these feasts in a very remarkable manner. Each of them used to eat a baked sheep and ten fowls dressed with sweetmeats, and ten pounds of sweetmeats besides, and was presented with a quantity of food carried away from the feast to his house, together with a large sum of money. One of them had been a prisoner at 'Askalán; and after he had remained there some time, the person into whose power he had fallen jestingly told him that if he would eat a calf belonging to him, the flesh of which weighed several hundredweights, he would emancipate him. This feat he accomplished and thus obtained his liberation.[1]

With respect to clean and unclean meats, the Muslim is subject to nearly the same laws as the Jew. Swine's flesh, and blood, are especially forbidden to him; but camel's flesh is allowed. The latter, however, being of a coarse nature, is never eaten when any other meat can be obtained, excepting by persons of the lower classes and by Arabs of the desert. Of fish, almost every kind is eaten (excepting shell-fish), usually fried in oil: of game, little; partly in consequence of frequent doubt whether it have been lawfully killed. The diet consists in a great measure

[1] El-Maḳreezee's Khiṭaṭ: Account of the Khaleefehs' Palaces.

of vegetables, and includes a large variety of pastry. A very common kind of pastry is a pancake, which is made very thin, and folded over several times like a napkin; it is saturated with butter, and generally sweetened with honey or sugar; as is also another common kind which somewhat resembles vermicelli.

The usual beverage at meals is water, which is drunk from cooling, porous, earthen bottles, or from cups of brass or other metal: but in the houses of the wealthy, sherbet is sometimes served instead of this, in covered glass cups, each of which contains about three-quarters of a pint. The sherbet is composed of water made very sweet with sugar, or with a hard conserve of violets or roses or mulberries. After every time that a person drinks, he says, "Praise be to God;" and each person of the company says to him, "May it be productive of enjoyment:" to which he replies, "May God cause thee to have enjoyment." The Arabs drink little or no water during a meal, but generally take a large draught immediately after. The repast is quickly finished; and each person, as soon as he has done, says, "Praise be to God," or "Praise be to God, the Lord of all creatures." He then washes in the same manner as before, but more thoroughly; well lathering his beard and rinsing his mouth.

"Whoever," said the Prophet, "believes in God and the day of resurrection, must respect his guest; and the time of being kind to him is one day and one night; and the period of entertaining him is three days; and after that, if he does it longer, he benefits him more; but it is not right for a guest to stay in the house of the host so long as to incommode him." He even allowed the "right of a guest" to be taken by force from such as would not offer it.[1] The following observations, respecting the treatment of guests by the Bedawees, present an interesting commentary upon the former precept:—"Strangers who have not any friend or acquaintance in the camp, alight at the first tent that presents itself: whether the owner be at home or not, the wife or daughter immediately spreads a carpet, and prepares breakfast or dinner. If the stranger's business requires a protracted stay, as, for instance, if he wishes to cross the Desert under the protection of the tribe, the host, after a lapse of three days and four hours from the time of his arrival, asks whether he means to honour him any longer with his company. If the stranger declares his intention of prolonging his visit, it is expected that he should assist his host in domestic matters, fetching water, milking the camel, feeding the horse, etc. Should he even decline this, he may remain; but he will be censured by all the Arabs of the camp: he may, however, go to some other tent of the nezel [or encampment], and declare himself there a guest. Thus, every third or fourth day he may change hosts,

[1] Mishkát el-Maṣábeeḥ, ii. 329.

until his business is finished, or he has reached his place of destination."[1]

The obligation which is imposed by eating another person's bread and salt, or salt alone, or eating such things with another, is well known; but the following example of it may be new to some readers.—Yaạḳoob the son of El-Leyth Eṣ-Ṣaffár, having adopted a predatory life, excavated a passage one night into the palace of Dirhem the Governor of Sijistán, or Seestán; and after he had "made up a convenient bale of gold and jewels, and the most costly stuffs, was proceeding to carry it off, when he happened in the dark to strike his foot against something hard on the floor. Thinking it might be a jewel of some sort or other, a diamond perhaps, he picked it up and put it to his tongue, and, to his equal mortification and disappointment, found it to be a lump of rock-salt; for having thus tasted the salt of the owner, his avarice gave way to his respect for the laws of hospitality; and throwing down his precious booty, he left it behind him, and withdrew empty-handed to his habitation. The treasurer of Dirhem repairing the next day, according to custom, to inspect his charge, was equally surprised and alarmed at observing that a great part of the treasure and other valuables had been removed; but on examining the package which lay on the floor, his astonishment was

[1] Burckhardt, Notes on the Bedouins and Wahábys, 8vo. ed. i. 178, 179.

not less, to find that not a single article had been conveyed away. The singularity of the circumstance induced him to report it immediately to his master: and the latter causing it to be proclaimed throughout the city, that the author of this proceeding had his free pardon, further announced that on repairing to the palace, he would be distinguished by the most encouraging marks of favour." Yaaḳoob availed himself of the invitation, relying upon the promise, which was fulfilled to him; and from this period he gradually rose in power until he became the founder of a Dynasty.[1]

In the houses of persons of the higher and middle classes in Cairo, the different apartments generally resemble each other in several respects and are similarly furnished. The greater portion of the floor is elevated about half a foot, or somewhat more, above the rest. The higher portion is called leewán (a corruption of "el-eewán"), and the lower, durḳá'ah, from the Persian dar-gáh. When there is but one leewán, the durḳá'ah occupies the lower end, extending from the door to the opposite wall. In a handsome house, it is usually paved with white and black marble and little pieces of red tile inlaid in tasteful and complicated patterns; and if the room is on the ground-floor, and sometimes in other cases, it has in the centre a fountain which plays into a small shallow

[1] Price's Retrospect of Mahom. History, ii. 229.

pool lined with coloured marbles like the surrounding pavement. The shoes or slippers are left upon the durḳá'ah previously to stepping upon the leewán. The latter is generally paved with common stone and covered with a mat in summer, and a carpet over this in winter; and a mattress and cushions are placed against each of its three walls, composing what is called a "deewán," or divan. The mattress, which is commonly about three feet wide and three or four inches thick, is placed either on the floor or on a raised frame or a slightly elevated pavement; and the cushions, which are usually of a length equal to the width of the mattress and of a height equal to half that measure, lean against the wall. Both mattresses and cushions are stuffed with cotton and are covered with printed calico, cloth, or some more expensive stuff. The deewán which extends along the upper end of the leewán is called the ṣadr, and is the most honourable: and the chief place on this seat is the corner which is to the right of a person facing this end of the room; the other corner is the next in point of honour; and the intermediate places on the same deewán are more honourable than those on the two side-deewáns. To a superior, and often to an equal, the master or mistress yields the chief place. The corners are often furnished with an additional mattress of a square form, just large enough for one person, placed upon the other mattress, and with two additional (but smaller) cushions to recline against. The walls are for the most part plastered and white-washed, and generally have two or more shallow cupboards, the doors of which, as well as those of the apartments, are fancifully constructed with small panels. The windows, which are chiefly composed of curious wooden lattice-work, serving to screen the inhabitants from the view of persons without, as also to admit both light and air, commonly project outwards, and are furnished with mattresses and cushions. In many houses there are, above these, small windows of coloured glass, representing bunches of flowers, etc. The ceiling is of wood, and certain portions of it, which are carved or otherwise ornamented by fanciful carpentry, are usually painted with bright colours, such as red, green, and blue, and sometimes varied with gilding; but the greater part of the wood-work is generally left unpainted.

The ḳá'ah is a large and lofty apartment, commonly having two leewáns on opposite sides of the durḳá'ah. One of these is in most instances larger than the other, and is held to be the more honourable part. Some ḳá'ahs, containing three leewáns, one of these being opposite the entrance, or four leewáns composing the form of a cross with the durḳá'ah in the centre, communicate with the small chambers or closets, or have elevated recesses which are furnished in the same manner as the leewáns. That part of the roof which is over the durḳá'ah rises above the rest, sometimes to nearly twice the height of the latter, and is generally surmounted by a lantern of wooden lattice-work to admit the air.

The prohibition of wine, or rather of fermented and intoxicating liquors, being one of the most remarkable and characteristic points of the Mohammadan religion, it might be imagined that the frequent stories in the "Thousand and One Nights," describing parties of Muslims as habitually indulging in the use of forbidden beverages, are scandalous misrepresentations of Arab manners and customs. There are, however, many similar anecdotes interspersed in the works of Arab historians, which (though many of them are probably untrue in their application to particular individuals) could not have been offered to the public by such writers if they were not of a nature consistent with the customs of a considerable class of the Arab nation.

In investigating this subject, it is necessary in the first place to state that there is a kind of wine which Muslims are permitted to drink. It is properly called nebeedh (a name which is *now* given to *prohibited* kinds of wine), and is generally prepared by putting dry grapes, or dry dates, in water, to extract their sweetness, and suffering the liquor to ferment slightly until it acquires a little sharpness or pungency. The Prophet himself was in the habit of drinking wine of this kind, which was prepared for him in the first part of the night; he drank it on the first and second days following; but if any remained on the morning of the third day, he either gave it to his servants or ordered it to be poured out upon the ground.[1] Such beverages have, therefore, been drunk by the strictest of his followers; and Ibn-Khaldoon strongly argues that nebeedh thus prepared from dates was the kind of wine used by the Khaleefehs Hároon Er-Rasheed and El-Ma-moon, and several other eminent men, who have been commonly accused of habitually and publicly indulging in debauches of wine properly so called, that is, of inebriating liquors.[2]

Nebeedh prepared from raisins is commonly sold in Arab towns under the name of "zebeeb," which signifies "raisins." This I have often drunk in Cairo, but never could perceive that it was in the slightest degree fermented. Other beverages, to which the name of "nebeedh" has been applied (though, like zebeeb, no longer called by that name), are also sold in Arab towns. The most common of these is an infusion of licorice, and called by the name of the root, 'erḳ-soos. The nebeedh of dates is sold in Cairo with the dates themselves in the liquor; and in like manner is that of figs. Under the same appellation of nebeedh have been classed the different kinds of beer now commonly called boozeh. Opium, hemp,

[1] Mishkát el-Maṣábeeḥ, ii. 339.
[2] De Sacy, Chrestomathie Arabe, i. 125–131, Arabic text.

etc., are now more frequently used by the Muslims to induce intoxication or exhilaration. The young leaves of the hemp are generally used alone, or mixed with tobacco, for smoking; and the capsules, without the seeds, enter into the composition of several intoxicating conserves.

By my own experience I am but little qualified to pronounce an opinion respecting the prevalence of drinking wine among the Arabs; for, never drinking it myself, I had little opportunity of observing others do so during my residence among Muslims. I judge, therefore, from the conversations and writings of Arabs, which justify me in asserting that the practice of drinking wine in private and by select parties is far from being uncommon among modern Muslims, though certainly more so than it was before the introduction of tobacco into the East, in the beginning of the seventeenth century of our era: for this herb, being in a slight degree exhilarating, and at the same time soothing, and unattended by the injurious effects that result from wine, is a sufficient luxury to many who, without it, would have recourse to intoxicating beverages merely to pass away hours of idleness. The use of coffee, too, which became common in Egypt, Syria, and other countries besides Arabia, a century earlier than tobacco, doubtless tended to render the habit of drinking wine less general. That it was adopted as a substitute for wine appears even from its name, "ḳahweh," an old Arabic term for wine; whence our "coffee."

There is an Arabic work of some celebrity, and not of small extent, entitled "Ḥalbet el-Kumeyt,"[1] apparently written shortly before the Arabs were in possession of the first of these substitutes for wine, nearly the whole of which consists of anecdotes and verses relating to the pleasures resulting from or attendant upon the use of wine; a few pages at the end being devoted to the condemnation of this practice, or, in other words, to proving the worthlessness of all that precedes. Of this work I possess a copy, a quarto volume of 464 pages. I have endeavoured to skim its cream; but found it impossible to do so without collecting at the same time a considerable quantity of most filthy scum; for it is characterised by wit and humour plentifully interlarded with the grossest and most revolting obscenity. Yet it serves to confirm what has been above asserted. The mere existence of such a work, (and it is not the only one of the kind,) written by a man of learning, and I believe a Ḳáḍee, (a judge,) or one holding the honourable office of a guardian of religion and morality,[2] and written evi-

[1] That is, a race-course for sallies of wit and eloquence on the subject of wine: the word "kumeyt" being used, in preference to more than a hundred others that might have been employed, to signify "wine," because it bears also the meaning of "a deep red horse." The book has been already quoted in these pages.

[2] His name is not mentioned in my copy; but D'Herbelot states

dently *con amore*, notwithstanding his assertion to the contrary,—is a strong argument in favour of the prevalence of the practice which it paints in the most fascinating colours, and then condemns. Its author terminates a chapter (the ninth), in which many well-known persons are mentioned as having been addicted to wine, by saying, that the Khaleefehs, Emeers, and Wezeers, so addicted, are too numerous to name in such a work; and by relating a story of a man who placed his own wife in pledge in the hands of a wine-merchant, after having expended in the purchase of the forbidden liquor all the property that he possessed. He excuses himself (in his preface) for writing this book, by saying that he had been ordered to do so by one whom he could not disobey; thus giving us a pretty strong proof that a great man in his own time was not ashamed of avowing his fondness for the prohibited enjoyment. If then we admit the respectable authority of Ibn-Khaldoon, and acquit of the vice of drunkenness those illustrious individuals whose characters he vindicates, we must still regard most of the anecdotes relating to the carousals of other persons as being not without foundation.

One of my friends, who enjoys a high reputation, ranking among the most distinguished of the 'Ulamà of Cairo, is well known to his intimate acquaintances

it to have been Shems-ed-Deen Moḥammad ibn-Bedr-ed-Deen Ḥasan el-Ḳáḍee; and writes his surname "Naouagi," or "Naouahi."

as frequently indulging in the use of forbidden beverages with a few select associates. I disturbed him and his companions by an evening visit on one of these occasions, and was kept waiting within the street door while the guests quickly removed everything that would give me any indication of the manner in which they had been employed; for the announcement of my (assumed) name,[1] and their knowledge of my abstemious character, completely disconcerted them. I found them, however, in the best humour. They had contrived, it appeared, to fill with wine a *china* bottle, of the kind used at that season (it was winter) for water; and when any one of them asked the servant for water, this bottle was brought to him; but when I made the same demand, my host told me that there was a bottle of water on the sill of the window behind that part of the deewán upon which I was seated. The evening passed away very pleasantly, and I should not have known how unwelcome was my intrusion had not one of the guests with whom I was intimately acquainted, in walking part of the way home with me, explained to me the whole occurrence. There was with us a third person, who, thinking that

[1] [Mr. Lane followed the usual custom of travellers of his day who wished to be intimate with the Egyptians, and took the name of Manṣoor Effendee. A letter from Bonomi to him, under this name, exists in the British Museum (25,658, f. 67), and has led the compilers of the Index to the Catalogue of Additions to the MSS., published in 1880, into the pardonable error of inventing an "Edward Mansoor Lane." S. L-P.]

my antipathy to wine was feigned, asked me to stop at his house on my way and take a cup of "white coffee," by which he meant brandy.

Another of my Muslim acquaintances in Cairo I frequently met at the house of a common friend, where, though he was in most respects very bigoted, he was in the habit of indulging in wine. For some time he refrained from this gratification when I was by; but at length my presence became so irksome to him that he ventured to enter into an argument with me on the subject of the prohibition. The only answer I could give to his question, "Why is wine forbidden?" was in the words of the Ḳur-án, "Because it is the source of more evil than profit."[1] This suited his purpose, as I intended it should; and he asked, "What evil results from it?" I answered, "Intoxication and quarrels, and so forth."—"Then," said he, "if a man take not enough to intoxicate him there is no harm;"—and, finding that I acquiesced by silence, he added, "I am in the habit of taking a little; but never enough to intoxicate. Boy, bring me a glass." He was the only Muslim, however, whom I have heard to argue against the absolute interdiction of inebriating liquors.

Histories tell us that some of the early followers of the Prophet indulged in wine, holding the text above referred to as indecisive; and that Moḥammad

[1] Ḳur. ii. 216.

was at first doubtful upon this subject appears from another text, in which his followers were told not to come to prayer when they were drunk, until they should know what they would say;[1] an injunction nearly similar to one in the Bible[2]: but when frequent and severe contentions resulted from their use of wine, the following more decided condemnation of the practice was pronounced:—"O ye who have become believers! verily wine and lots and images and divining-arrows are an abomination of the work of the Devil; therefore, avoid them, that ye may prosper."[3] This law is absolute; its violation in the smallest degree is criminal. The punishment ordained by the law for drinking (or, according to most doctors, for even tasting) wine or spirits, or inducing intoxication by any other means, on ordinary occasions, is the infliction of eighty stripes in the case of a free man, and forty in that of a slave: but if the crime be openly committed in the course of any day of the month of Ramaḍán, when others are fasting, the punishment prescribed is death!

The prohibition of wine hindered many of the Prophet's contemporaries from embracing his religion. It is said that the famous poet El-Aạshà, who was one of them, delayed to join this cause on this account, until death prevented him. A person passing by his tomb (at Menfooḥah, in El-Yemámeh), and observing

[1] Ḳur. iv. 46. [2] Lev. x. 9. [3] Ḳur. v. 92.

that it was moist, asked the reason, and was answered that the young men of the place, considering him still as their cup-companion, drank wine over his grave, and poured his cup upon it.[1]

Yet many of the most respectable of the pagan Arabs, like certain of the Jews and early Christians, abstained totally from wine, from a feeling of its injurious effects upon morals, and, in their climate, upon health; or more especially from the fear of being led by it into the commission of foolish and degrading actions. Thus, Ḳeys the son of Áṣim being one night overcome with wine attempted to grasp the moon, and swore that he would not quit the spot where he stood until he had laid hold of it: after leaping several times with the view of doing so, he fell flat upon his face; and when he recovered his senses, and was acquainted with the cause of his face being bruised, he made a solemn vow to abstain from wine ever after.[2] A similar feeling operated upon many Muslims more than religious principle. The Khaleefeh 'Abd-El-Melik Ibn-Marwán took pleasure in the company of a slave named Naṣeeb, and one day desired him to drink with him. The slave replied, "O Prince of the Faithful, I am not related to thee, nor have I any authority over thee, and I am of no rank or lineage; I am a black slave, and my wit and politeness have drawn me into thy favour: how then

[1] Ḥalbet el-Kumeyt, chap. ix. [2] Ibid, khátimeh.

shall I take that which will plunder me of these two qualities, and by what shall I then propitiate thee?" The Khaleefeh admired and excused him.[1]

It was the custom of many Muslim princes, as might be inferred from the above anecdote, to admit the meanest of their dependants to participate in their unlawful carousals when they could have no better companions; but poets and musicians were their more common associates on these occasions; and these two classes, and especially the latter, are in the present day the most addicted to intoxicating liquors. Few modern Arab musicians are so well contented with extraordinary payment and mere sweet sherbet as with a moderate fee and plenty of wine and brandy; and many of them deem even wine but a sorry beverage.

It was usual with the host and guests at wine-parties to wear dresses of bright colours, red, yellow, and green;[2] and to perfume their beards and mustaches with civet, or to have rose-water sprinkled upon them; and ambergris or aloes-wood, or some other odoriferous substance, placed upon burning coals in a censer, diffused a delicious fragrance throughout the saloon of the revels.

The wine, it appears, was rather thick, for it was necessary to strain it:[3] it was probably sweet, and not

[1] Ḥalbet el-Kumeyt, l.l.

[2] Fakhr-ed-Deen, in De Sacy, Chrest. Arabe.

[3] "While tears of blood trickle from the strainer, the ewer beneath

strong, for it was drunk in large quantities. In general, perhaps, it was nebeedh of dry raisins kept longer than the law allows. It was usually kept in a large earthen vessel, called denn, high, and small at the bottom, which was partly imbedded in the earth to keep it upright. The name of this vessel is now given to a cask of wood; but the kind above mentioned was of earth, for it was easily broken. A famous saint, Abu-l-Ḥoseyn En-Nooree, seeing a vessel on the Tigris containing thirty denns belonging to the Khaleefeh El-Moạtaḍid, and beïng told that they contained wine, took a boat-pole, and broke them all, save one. When brought before the Khaleefeh to answer for this action, and asked by him, "Who made thee Moḥtesib?"[1] he boldly answered, "He who made thee Khaleefeh!"—and was pardoned.[2]

Pitch was used by the Arabs, as it was by the Greeks and Romans, for the purpose of curing their wine; the interior of the denn being coated with it. A smaller kind of earthen jar, or amphora (báṭiyeh), and a bottle of leather (baṭṭah), or of glass (kinneeneh), were also used. The wine was transferred for the table to glass jugs, or long-spouted ewers (ibreeḳs). These and the cups were placed upon a round embroidered

it giggles." (Eṣ-Ṣadr Ibn-El-Wekeel, quoted in the Ḥalbet el-Kumeyt, chap. xiii.)—The strainer is called "ráwooḳ."

[1] The Moḥtesib is inspector of the markets, the weights and measures, and provisions, etc.

[2] Mir-át ez-Zemán, events of the year 295.

cloth spread on the floor, or upon a round tray. The latter is now in general use, and is supported on the low stool already described as being used at ordinary meals. The guests sat around, reclining against pillows; or they sat upon the deewán, and a page or slave handed the cup, having on his right arm a richly embroidered napkin, on the end of which the drinker wiped his lips. The cups are often described as holding a fluid pound, or little less than an English pint, and this is to be understood literally, or nearly so: they were commonly of cut glass, but some were of crystal or silver or gold.[1] With these and the ewers or jugs were placed several saucers, or small dishes (nuḳuldáns), of fresh and dried fruits (nuḳl); and fans and fly-whisks, of the kind described on a former occasion, were used by the guests.

The most common and esteemed fruits in the countries inhabited by the Arabs may here be mentioned.

The date (belaḥ) deserves the first place. The Prophet's favourite fruits were fresh dates (ruṭab) and water-melons; and he ate them both together.[2]

[1] The cup, when full, was generally called "kás:" when empty, "ḳadaḥ," or "jám." The name of kás is now given to a small glass used for brandy and liqueurs, and similar to our liqueur-glass: the glass or cup used for wine is called, when so used, "koobeh:" it is the same as that used for sherbet; but in the latter case it is called "ḳulleh."

[2] Es-Suyooṭee, account of the fruits of Egypt, in his history of that country (MS.)

"Honour," said he, "your paternal aunt, the date-palm; for she was created of the earth of which Adam was formed."[1] It is said that God hath given this tree as a peculiar favour to the Muslims; that he hath decreed all the date-palms in the world to them, and they have accordingly conquered every country in which these trees are found; and all are said to have derived their origin from the Ḥijáz.[2] The palm-tree has several well-known properties that render it an emblem of a human being; among which are these: that if the head be cut off, the tree dies; and if a branch be cut off, another does not grow in its place.[3] Dates are preserved in a moist state by being merely pressed together in a basket or skin, and thus prepared are called 'ajweh. There are many varieties of this fruit. The pith or heart of the palm (jummár) is esteemed for its delicate flavour.

The water-melon (biṭṭeekh, vulg. baṭṭeekh), from what has been said of it above, ought to be ranked next; and it really merits this distinction. "Whoso eateth," said the Prophet, "a mouthful of water-melon, God writeth for him a thousand good works, and cancelleth a thousand evil works, and raiseth him a thousand degrees; for it came from Paradise;"—and again, "The water-melon is food and drink, acid and alkali, and a support of life," etc.[4] The varieties of this fruit are very numerous.

[1] Es Suyooṭee. [2] Ibid. [3] El-Ḳazweenee, MS. [4] Ibid.

The banana (móz) is a delicious fruit. The Prophet pronounced the banana-tree to be the only thing on earth that resembles a thing in Paradise, because it bears fruit both in winter and summer.[1]

The pomegranate (rummán) is another celebrated fruit. Every pomegranate, according to the Prophet, contains a fecundating seed from Paradise.[2]

The other most common and esteemed fruits are the following;—the apple, pear, quince, apricot, peach, fig, sycamore-fig, grape, lote, jujube, plum, walnut, almond, hazel-nut, pistachio-nut, orange, Seville orange, lime lemon, citron, mulberry, olive, and sugar-cane.[3]

Of a selection of these fruits consists the dessert which accompanies the wine; but the table is not complete without a bunch or two of flowers placed in the midst.

Though the Arabs are far from being remarkable for exhibiting taste in the planning of their gardens, they are passionately fond of flowers, and especially of the rose (ward). The Khaleefeh El-Mutawekkil monopolized roses for his own enjoyment; saying, "I am the King of Sulṭáns, and the rose is the king of sweet-scented flowers; therefore each of us is most

[1] Es-Suyooṭee, ubi supra. [2] Ibid.

[3] The Arabic names of these fruits are, tuffáḥ (vulgo, tiffáḥ) kummetrè, safarjal, mishmish, khókh, teen, jummeyz (vulgo, jemmeyz), 'eneb, nabḳ or sidr, 'onnáb (vulgo, 'annáb), ijjás or barḳooḳ, józ, lóz, bunduḳ, fustuḳ, burtuḳán, nárinj, leymoon, utrujj or turunj, kebbád, toot, zeytoon, and ḳaṣab es-sukkar.

worthy of the other for a companion." The rose in his time was seen nowhere but in his palace: during the season of this flower he wore rose-coloured clothes; and his carpets were sprinkled with rose-water.[1] A similar passion for the rose is said to have distinguished a weaver in the reign of El-Ma-moon. He was constantly employed at his loom every day of the year, even during the congregational-prayers of Friday, excepting in the rose-season, when he abandoned his work and gave himself up to the enjoyment of wine early in the morning and late in the evening, loudly proclaiming his revels by singing,—

"The season has become pleasant! The time of the rose is come! Take your morning potations, as long as the rose has blossoms and flowers!"

When he resumed his work, he made it known by singing aloud—

"If my Lord prolong my life until the rose-season, I will take again my morning potations: but if I die before it, alas! for the loss of the rose and wine!

"I implore the God of the supreme throne, whose glory be extolled, that my heart may continually enjoy the evening potations to the day of resurrection."

The Khaleefeh was so amused with the humour of this man that he granted him an annual pension of ten thousand dirhems to enable him to enjoy himself amply on these occasions. Another anecdote

[1] Ḥalbet el-Kumeyt, chap. xvii.; and Es-Suyooṭee, account of the flowers of Egypt, in his history of that country.

may be added to show the estimation of the rose in the mind of an Arab. It is said that Rowḥ Ibn-Ḥátim, the governor of the province of Northern Africa, was sitting one day, with a female slave, in an apartment of his palace, when a eunuch brought him a jar full of red and white roses which a man had offered as a present. He ordered the eunuch to fill the jar with silver in return; but his slave said, "O my lord, thou hast not acted equitably towards the man; for his present to thee is of two colours, red and white." The Emeer replied, "Thou hast said truly;" and gave orders to fill the jar for him with silver and gold (dirhems and deenárs) intermixed. Some persons preserve roses during the whole of the year in the following manner. They take a number of rose-buds and fill with them a new earthen jar, and, after closing its mouth with mud so as to render it impervious to the air, bury it in the earth. Whenever they want a few roses, they take out some of these buds, which they find unaltered, sprinkle a little water upon them and leave them for a short time in the air, when they open and appear as if just gathered.[1]

The rose is even a subject of miracles. It is related by Ibn-Ḳuteybeh that there grows in India a kind of rose, upon the leaves of which is inscribed, "There is no deity but God:"[2] But I

[1] Ḥalbet el-Kumeyt, chap. xvii.

[2] Ibid.

find a more particular account of this miraculous rose. A person, who professed to have seen it, said, "I went into India, and I saw at one of its towns a large rose, sweet-scented, upon which was inscribed, in white characters, 'There is no deity but God; Moḥammad is God's apostle: Aboo-Bekr is the very veracious: 'Omar is the discriminator:' and I doubted of this, whether it had been done by art; so I took one of the blossoms not yet opened, and in it was the same inscription; and there were many of the same kind there. The people of that place worshipped stones, and knew not God, to whom be ascribed might and glory."[1] Roses are announced for sale in the streets of Cairo by the cry of "The rose was a thorn: from the sweat of the Prophet it blossomed!" in allusion to a miracle recorded of Moḥammad. "When I was taken up into heaven," said the Prophet, "some of my sweat fell upon the earth, and from it sprang the rose; and whoever would smell my scent, let him smell the rose." In another tradition it is said, "The white rose was created from my sweat on the night of the Meạráj;[2] and the red rose, from the sweat of Jebraeel;[3] and the yellow rose, from the sweat of El-Buráḳ."[4] The Persians take especial delight in

[1] Es-Suyooṭee, ubi supra.

[2] The night of the Prophet's Ascension [in dream, into Heaven].

[3] Gabriel, who accompanied the Prophet.

[4] The beast on which Moḥammad dreamed he rode from Mekkeh

roses; sometimes spreading them as carpets or beds on which to sit or recline in their revellings.

But there is a flower pronounced more excellent than the rose, that of the Egyptian privet, or Lawsonia inermis.[1] Moḥammad said, "The chief of the sweet-scented flowers of this world and of the next is the fághiyeh;" and this was his favourite flower.[2] I approve of his taste; for this flower, which grows in clusters somewhat like those of the lilac, has a most delicious fragrance. But, on account of discrepancies in different traditions, a Muslim may with a clear conscience prefer either of the two flowers next mentioned.

The Prophet said of the violet (benefsej), "The excellence of the extract of violets, above all other extracts, is as the excellence of me above all the rest of the creation: it is cold in summer, and hot in winter:" and, in another tradition, "The excellence of the violet is as the excellence of el-Islám above all other religions."[3] A delicious sherbet is made of a conserve of sugar and violet-flowers.

The myrtle (ás or narseen) is the rival of the

to Jerusalem previously to his ascension. These traditions are from Es-Suyooṭee, ubi supra.

[1] This flower is called "fághiyeh," and more commonly "temer el-ḥennà;" or, according to some, the fághiyeh is the flower produced by a slip of temer el-ḥennà, planted upside down, and superior to the flower of the latter planted in the natural way!

[2] Es-Suyooṭee, ubi supra. [3] Ibid.

violet. "Adam," said the Prophet, "fell down from Paradise with three things; the myrtle, which is the chief of sweet-scented flowers in this world; an ear of wheat, which is the chief of all kinds of food in this world; and pressed dates, which are the chief of the fruits of this world."[1]

The anemone[2] was monopolized for his own enjoyment by Noamán Ibn-El-Mundhir (King of El-Ḥeereh, and contemporary of Moḥammad), as the rose was afterwards by El-Mutawekkil.[3]

Another flower much admired and celebrated in the East is the gilliflower (menthoor or kheeree). There are three principal kinds; the most esteemed is the yellow, or gold-coloured, which has a delicious scent both by night and day; the next, the purple, and other dark kinds, which have a scent only in the night; the least esteemed, the white, which has no scent. The yellow gilliflower is an emblem of a neglected lover.[4]

The narcissus (narjis) is very highly esteemed. Galen says, "He who has two cakes of bread, let him dispose of one of them for some flowers of the narcissus; for bread is the food of the body, and the

[1] Es-Suyooṭee.

[2] Shaḳáïḳ. The "adhriyoon," or "ádharyoon," is said to be a variety of the anemone.

[3] From the former, or from "noamán," signifying "blood," the anemone was named "shaḳáïḳ en-noamán."

[4] Ḥalbet el-Kumeyt, chap. xvii.

narcissus is the food of the soul." Hippocrates gave a similar opinion.[1]

The following flowers complete the list of those celebrated as most appropriate to add to the delights of wine :—the jasmine, eglantine, Seville-orange-flower, lily, sweet-basil, wild thyme, buphthalmum, chamomile, nenuphar, lotus, pomegranate-flower, poppy, ketmia, crocus or saffron, safflower, flax, the blossoms of different kinds of bean, and those of the almond.[2]

A sprig of Oriental willow[3] adds much to the charms of a bunch of flowers, being the favourite symbol of a graceful woman.

But I have not yet mentioned all that contributes to the pleasures of an Eastern carousal. For what is the juice of the grape without melodious sounds? "Wine is as the body; music, as the soul; and joy is their offspring."[4] All the five senses should be gratified. For this reason an Arab toper, who had nothing, it appears, but wine to enjoy, exclaimed,—

"Ho! give me wine to drink; and tell me 'This is wine;'"

---

[1] Ḥalbet el-Kumeyt; Es-Suyooṭee, ubi supra; and El-Ḳazweenee.

[2] The Arabic names of these flowers are, yásameen, nisreen, zaḥr (or zahr nárinj), soosan, reeḥán (or ḥobaḳ), nemám, bahár, uḳḥowán, neelófar, beshneen, jullanár or julnár, khashkhásh, khiṭmee, zaạfarán, 'oṣfur, kettán, báḳillà and lebláb, and lóz.

[3] Bán, and khiláf or khaláf. Both these names are applied to the same tree (which, according to Forskal, differs slightly from the salix Ægyptiaca of Linnæus) by the author of the Ḥalbet el-Kumeyt and by the modern Egyptians.

[4] Ḥalbet el-Kumeyt, chap. xiv.

for in drinking his sight and smell and taste and touch would all be affected; but it was desirable that his hearing should also be pleased.[1]

Music was condemned by the Prophet almost as severely as wine. "Singing and hearing songs," said he, "cause hypocrisy to grow in the heart, like as water promoteth the growth of corn:"[2]—and musical instruments he declared to be among the most powerful means by which the Devil seduces man. An instrument of music is the Devil's muëddin, serving to call men to his worship. Of the hypocrisy of those attached to music, the following anecdote presents an instance:—A drunken young man with a lute in his hand was brought one night before the Khaleefeh 'Abd-El-Melik the son of Marwán, who, pointing to the instrument, asked what it was, and what was its use. The youth made no answer; so he asked those around him; but they also remained silent, till one, more bold than the rest, said, "O Prince of the Faithful, this is a lute: it is made by taking some wood of the pistachio-tree, and cutting it into thin pieces, and gluing these together, and then attaching over them these chords, which, when a beautiful girl touches them, send forth sounds more pleasant than those of rain falling upon a desert land; and my wife be separated from me by a triple divorce,

[1] Ḥalbet el-Kumeyt, chap. xi.
[2] Mishkát el-Maṣábeeḥ, ii. 425.

if every one in this council is not acquainted with it, and doth not know it as well as I do, and thou the first of them, O Prince of the Faithful." The Khaleefeh laughed, and ordered that the young man should be discharged.[1]

The latter saying of the Prophet, respecting the Devil, suggests another anecdote related of himself by Ibraheem El-Mósilee, the father of Isháḳ; both of whom were very celebrated musicians. I give a translation of it somewhat abridged.—"I asked Er-Rasheed," says Ibraheem, "to grant me permission to spend a day at home with my women and brothers; and he gave me two thousand deenárs, and appointed the next Saturday for this purpose. I caused the meats and wine and other necessaries to be prepared, and ordered the chamberlain to close the door, and admit no one: but while I was sitting, with my attendants standing in the form of a curved line before me, there entered and approached me a sheykh, reverend and dignified and comely in appearance, wearing short khuffs,[2] and two soft gowns, with a ḳalensuweh [sugar-loaf hat] upon his head, and in his hand a silver-headed staff; and sweet odours were diffused from his clothes. I was enraged with the chamberlain for admitting him; but on his saluting me in a very courteous manner, I returned his saluta-

[1] Ḥalbet el-Kumeyt, chap. xiv.

[2] Soft boots, worn inside the slippers or shoes.

tion, and desired him to sit down. He then began to repeat to me stories, tales of war, and poetry; so that my anger was appeased, and it appeared to me that my servants had not presumed to admit him until acquainted with his politeness and courteousness. I therefore said to him, 'Hast thou any inclination for meat?' He answered, 'I have no want of it.'—'And the wine?' said I. He replied, 'Yes.' So I drank a large cupful, and he did the same, and then said to me, 'O Ibraheem, wilt thou let us hear some specimen of thy art in which thou hast excelled the people of thy profession?' I was angry at his words; but I made light of the matter, and, having taken the lute and tuned it, I played and sang; whereupon he said, 'Thou hast performed well, O Ibraheem.' I became more enraged, and said within myself, 'He is not content with coming hither without permission, and asking me to sing, but he calls me by my name, and proves himself unworthy of my conversation.' He then said, 'Wilt thou let us hear more? If so we will requite thee.' And I took the lute and sang, using my utmost care on account of his saying, 'we will requite thee.' He was moved with delight, and said, 'Thou hast performed well, O my master Ibraheem:'—adding, 'Wilt thou permit thy slave to sing?' I answered, 'As thou pleasest:'—but thinking lightly of his sense to sing after me. He took the lute, and tuned it; and, by Allah! I imagined that the lute spoke in his hands with an eloquent Arab tongue. He proceeded to sing some verses commencing,—

'My heart is wounded! Who will give me for it a heart without a wound?'"

The narrator continues by saying that he was struck dumb and motionless with ecstasy; and that the strange sheykh, after having played and sung again, and taught him an enchanting air (with which he afterwards enraptured his patron, the Khaleefeh), vanished. Ibraheem, in alarm, seized his sword; and was the more amazed when he found that the porter had not seen the stranger enter or leave the house; but he heard his voice again, outside, telling him that he was Aboo-Murrah (the Devil).[1]

Ibraheem El-Mósilee, his son Isḥáḳ, and Mukháriḳ[2] (a pupil of the former), were especially celebrated among Arab musicians and among the distinguished men of the reign of Hároon Er-Rasheed. Isḥáḳ El-Móṣilee relates of his father Ibraheem that when Er-Rasheed took him into his service he gave him a hundred and fifty thousand dirhems and allotted him a monthly pension of ten thousand dirhems, besides occasional presents [one of which is mentioned as amounting to a hundred thousand dirhems for a

[1] Ḥalbet el-Kumeyt, chap. xiv.

[2] I am not sure of the orthography of this name, particularly with respect to the first and last vowels; having never found it written with the vowel-points. It is sometimes written with ḥ for kh, and f for ḳ.

single song], and the produce of his (Ibraheem's) farms: he had food constantly prepared for him; three sheep every day for his kitchen, besides birds; three thousand dirhems were allowed him for fruits, perfumes, etc., every month, and a thousand dirhems for his clothing; "and with all this," says his son, "he died without leaving more than three thousand deenárs, a sum not equal to his debts, which I paid after his death."[1] Ibraheem was of Persian origin, and of a high family. He was commonly called the Nedeem (or cup-companion), being Er-Rasheed's favourite companion at the wine-table; and his son, who enjoyed the like distinction with El-Ma-moon, received the same appellation, as well as that of "Son of the Nedeem." Ibraheem was the most famous musician of his time, at least till his son attained celebrity.[2]

Isḥáḳ El-Mósilee was especially famous as a musician; but he was also a good poet, accomplished in general literature, and endowed with great wit. He was honoured above all other persons in the pay of El-Ma-moon, and enjoyed a long life; but for many years before his death he was blind.[3]

Mukháriḳ appears to have rivalled his master Ibraheem. The latter, he relates, took him to perform before Er-Rasheed, who used to have a curtain sus-

[1] Ḥalbet el-Kumeyt, l.l.

[2] He was born in A.H. 125, and died in 213, or 188.

[3] He was born A.H. 150, and died in 235.

pended between him and the musicians. "Others," he says, "sang, and he was unmoved; but when I sang, he came forth from behind the curtain, and exclaimed, 'Young man, hither!' and he seated me upon the couch (sereer) and gave me thirty thousand dirhems."[1] The following anecdote (which I abridge a little in translation) shows his excellence in the art which he professed, and the effect of melody on an Arab:—"After drinking with the Khaleefeh [El-Mamoon, I think,] a whole night, I asked his permission," says he, "to take the air in the Ruṣáfeh [quarter of Baghdád], which he granted; and while I was walking there, I saw a damsel who appeared as if the rising sun beamed from her face. She had a basket, and I followed her. She stopped at a fruiterer's, and bought some fruit; and observing that I was following her, she looked back and abused me several times; but still I followed her until she arrived at a great door, after having filled her basket with fruits and flowers and similar things. When she had entered and the door was closed behind her, I sat down opposite to it, deprived of my reason by her beauty; and knew that there must be in the house a wine party.

"The sun went down upon me while I sat there; and at length there came two handsome young men on asses, and they knocked at the door, and when they were admitted, I entered with them; the master of

[1] Mir-át ez-Zemán, events of the year 231. He died in this year.

the house thinking that I was their companion, and they imagining that I was one of his friends. A repast was brought up, and we ate, and washed our hands, and were perfumed. The master of the house then said to the two young men, 'Have ye any desire that I should call such a one?' (mentioning a woman's name). They answered, 'If thou wilt grant us the favour, well:'—so he called for her, and she came, and lo, she was the maiden whom I had seen before, and who had abused me. A servant-maid preceded her, bearing her lute, which she placed in her lap. Wine was then brought, and she sang, while we drank, and shook with delight. 'Whose air is that?' they asked. She answered, 'My master Mukhárik's.' She then sang another air, which she said was also mine; while they drank by pints; she looking aside and doubtfully at me until I lost my patience, and called out to her to do her best: but in attempting to do so, singing a third air, she overstrained her voice, and I said, 'Thou hast made a mistake:'—upon which she threw the lute from her lap in anger, so that she nearly broke it, saying, 'Take it thyself, and let us hear thee.' I answered, 'Well;' and, having taken it and tuned it perfectly, sang the first of the airs which she had sung before me; whereupon all of them sprang upon their feet and kissed my head. I then sang the second air, and the third; and their reason almost fled with ecstasy.

"The master of the house, after asking his guests and being told by them that they knew me not, came to me, and, kissing my hand, said, 'By Allah, my master, who art thou?' I answered, 'By Allah, I am the singer Mukhárik.'—'And for what purpose,' said he, kissing both my hands, 'camest thou hither?' I replied, 'As a spunger;'—and related what had happened with respect to the maiden: whereupon he looked towards his two companions and said to them, 'Tell me, by Allah, do ye not know that I gave for that girl thirty thousand dirhems, and have refused to sell her?' They answered, 'It is so.' Then said he, 'I take you as witnesses that I have given her to him.'—'And we,' said the two friends, 'will pay thee two-thirds of her price.' So he put me in possession of the girl, and in the evening when I departed, he presented me also with rich dresses and other gifts, with all of which I went away; and as I passed the places where the maiden had abused me, I said to her, 'Repeat thy words to me;' but she could not for shame. Holding the girl's hand, I went with her immediately to the Khaleefeh, whom I found in anger at my long absence; but when I related my story to him he was surprised, and laughed, and ordered that the master of the house and his two friends should be brought before him, that he might requite them; to the former he gave forty thousand dirhems; to each of his two friends, thirty thousand; and to me a hundred thousand; and I kissed his feet and departed."[1]

It is particularly necessary for the Arab musician that he have a retentive memory, well stocked with choice pieces of poetry and with facetious or pleasant anecdotes, interspersed with songs; and that he have a ready wit, aided by dramatic talent, to employ these materials with good effect. If to such qualifications he adds fair attainments in the difficult rules of grammar, a degree of eloquence, comic humour, and good temper, and is not surpassed by many in his art, he is sure to be a general favourite. Very few Muslims of the higher classes have condescended to study music, because they would have been despised by their inferiors for doing so; or because they themselves have despised or condemned the art. Ibraheem, the son of the Khaleefeh El-Mahdee, and competitor of El-Ma-moon, was a remarkable exception: he is said to have been an excellent musician and a good singer.

In the houses of the wealthy, the vocal and instrumental performers were usually (as is the case in many houses in the present age) domestic female slaves, well instructed in their art by hired male or female professors. In the "Thousand and One Nights," these slaves are commonly described as standing or sitting unveiled in the presence of male guests; but from

[1] Ḥalbet el-Kumeyt, chap. vii.

several descriptions of musical entertainments that I have met with in Arabic works it appears that according to the more approved custom in respectable society they were concealed on such occasions behind a curtain which generally closed the front of an elevated recess. In all the houses of wealthy Arabs that I have entered, one or each of the larger saloons has an elevated closet, the front of which is closed by a screen of wooden lattice-work to serve as an orchestra for the domestic or hired female singers and instrumental performers.

To a person acquainted with modern Arabian manners, it must appear inconsistent with truth to describe (as is often the case in the "Thousand and One Nights") such female singers as exposing their faces before strange men, unless he can discover in sober histories some evidence of their having been less strict in this respect than the generality of Arab women at the present time. I find, however, a remarkable proof that such was the case in the latter part of the ninth century of the Flight, and the beginning of the tenth: that is, about the end of the fifteenth century of our era. The famous historian Es-Suyooṭee, who flourished at this period, in his preface to a curious work on wedlock, written to correct the corrupt manners of his age, says:—"Seeing that the women of this time deck themselves with the attire of wantons, and walk in the sooḳs (or market-streets) like female warriors against the religion, and uncover their faces and hands before men to incline (men's) hearts to them by evil suggestions, and play at feasts with young men, thereby meriting the anger of the Compassionate [God], and go forth to the public baths and assemblies with various kinds of ornaments and perfumes and with conceited gait; (for the which they shall be congregated in Hell-fire, for opposing the good and on account of this their affected gait;) while to their husbands they are disobedient, behaving to them in the reverse manner, excepting when they fear to abridge their liberty of going abroad by such conduct; for they are like swine and apes in their interior nature, though like daughters of Adam in their exterior appearance; especially the women of this age; not advising their husbands in matters of religion, but the latter erring in permitting them to go out to every assembly; sisters of devils and demons, etc. etc. . . . . I have undertaken the composition of this volume."[1] A more convincing testimony than this, I think, cannot be required.

The lute (el-'ood) is the only instrument that is generally described as used at the entertainments which we have been considering. Engravings of this and other musical instruments are given in my work on the Modern Egyptians. The Arab viol (called rabáb) was commonly used by inferior performers.

The Arab music is generally of a soft and plaintive

[1] Nuzhet el-Mutaämmil.

character, and particularly that of the most refined description, which is distinguished by a peculiar system of intervals. The singer aims at distinct enunciation of the words, for this is justly admired; and delights in a trilling style. The airs of songs are commonly very short and simple, adapted to a single verse, or even to a single hemistich; but in the instrumental music there is more variety.

Scarcely less popular as an amusement and mode of passing the time is the bath, or hammám,—a favourite resort of both men and women of all classes among the Muslims who can afford the trifling expense which it requires; and (it is said) not only of human beings, but also of evil genii; on which account, as well as on that of decency, several precepts respecting it have been dictated by Moḥammad. It is frequented for the purpose of performing certain ablutions required by the religion, or by a regard for cleanliness, for its salutary effects, and for mere luxury.

The following description of a public bath will convey a sufficient notion of those in private houses, which are on a smaller scale and generally consist of only two or three chambers. The public bath comprises several apartments with mosaic or tesselated pavements, composed of white and black marble and pieces of fine red tile and sometimes other materials. The inner apartments are covered with domes, having a number of small round glazed apertures for the admission of light. The first apartment is the meslakh, or disrobing room, which has in the centre a fountain of cold water, and next the walls wide benches or platforms encased with marble. These are furnished with mattresses and cushions for the higher and middle classes, and with mats for the poorer sort. The inner division of the building, in the more regularly planned baths, occupies nearly a square: the central and chief portion of it is the principal apartment, or ḥarárah, which generally has the form of a cross. In its centre is a fountain of hot water, rising from a base encased with marble, which serves as a seat. One of the angles of the square is occupied by the beyt-owwal, or ante-chamber of the ḥarárah: in another is the fire over which is the boiler; and each of the other two angles is generally occupied by two small chambers, in one of which is a tank filled with warm water, which pours down from a spot in the dome; in the other, two taps side by side, one of hot and the other of cold water, with a small trough beneath, before which is a seat. The inner apartments are heated by the steam which rises from the fountain and tanks, and by the contiguity of the fire; but the beyt-owwal is not so hot as the ḥarárah, being separated from it by a door. In cold weather the bather undresses in the former, which has two or three raised seats like those of the meslakh.

With a pair of wooden clogs to his feet, and having a large napkin round his loins, and generally a second wound round his head like a turban, a third over his chest, and a fourth covering his back, the bather enters the ḥarárah, the heat of which causes him immediately to perspire profusely. An attendant of the bath removes from him all the napkins excepting the first; and proceeds to crack the joints of his fingers and toes, and several of the vertebrae of the back and neck; kneads his flesh, and rubs the soles of his feet with a coarse earthen rasp, and his limbs and body with a woollen bag which covers his hand as a glove; after which, the bather, if he please, plunges into one of the tanks. He is then thoroughly washed with soap and water and fibres of the palm-tree, and shaved, if he wish it, in one of the small chambers which contain the taps of hot and cold water; and returns to the beyt-owwal. Here he generally reclines upon a mattress, and takes some light refreshment, while one of the attendants rubs the soles of his feet and kneads the flesh of his body and limbs, previously to his resuming his dress. It is a common custom now to take a pipe and a cup of coffee during this period of rest.

The women are especially fond of the bath, and often have entertainments there; taking with them fruits, sweetmeats, etc., and sometimes hiring female singers to accompany them. An hour or more is occupied by the process of plaiting the hair and applying the depilatory, etc.; and generally an equal time is passed in the enjoyment of rest or recreation or refreshment. All necessary decorum is observed on these occasions by most ladies, but women of the lower orders are often seen in the bath without any covering. Some baths are appropriated solely to men; others, only to women; and others, again, to men during the forenoon, and in the afternoon to women. When the bath is appropriated to women, a napkin, or some other piece of drapery is suspended over the door to warn men from entering.

Before the time of Moḥammad, there were no public baths in Arabia; and he was so prejudiced against them, for reasons already alluded to, that he at first forbade both men and women from entering them: afterwards, however, he permitted men to do so, if for the sake of cleanliness, on the condition of their wearing a cloth; and women also on account of sickness, child-birth, etc., provided they had not convenient places for bathing in their houses. But notwithstanding this license, it is held to be a characteristic of a virtuous woman not to go to a bath even with her husband's permission: for the Prophet said, "Whatever woman enters a bath, the devil is with her." As the bath is a resort of the Jinn, prayer should not be performed in it, nor the Ḳur-án recited. The Prophet said, "All the earth is given to me as a place of prayer, and as pure, except the burial-ground and the bath." Hence also, when a person is about to enter a bath, he should offer up an ejaculatory prayer for protection against evil spirits; and should place his left foot first over the threshold. Infidels have often been obliged to distinguish themselves in the bath, by hanging a signet to the neck, or wearing anklets, etc., lest they should receive those marks of respect which should be paid only to believers.[1]

Hunting and hawking, which were common and favourite diversions of the Arabs, and especially of their kings and other great men, have now fallen into comparative disuse among this people. They are, however, still frequently practised by the Persians, and in the same manner as they are generally described in the "Thousand and One Nights."[2] The more common kinds of game are gazelles, or antelopes, hares, partridges, the species of grouse called "ḳaṭà," quails, wild geese, ducks, etc. Against all of these, the hawk is generally employed, but assisted in the capture of gazelles and hares by dogs. The usual arms of the sportsmen in mediæval times were the bow and arrow, the cross-bow, the spear, the sword and the mace. When the game is struck down but not killed by any weapon, its throat is immediately cut. If merely stunned and then left to die, its flesh is unlawful food. Hunting is allowable only for the purpose of procuring food, or to obtain the skin of an

[1] Nuzhet el-Mutaämmil, section vii.

[2] See Sir John Malcolm's "Sketches in Persia," i. ch. v.

animal, or for the sake of destroying ferocious and dangerous beasts; but the rule is often disregarded. Amusement is certainly, in general, the main object of the Muslim huntsman; but he does not with this view endeavour to prolong the chase; on the contrary, he strives to take the game as quickly as possible. For this purpose nets are often employed, and the hunting party, forming what is called the circle of the chase (ḥalḳat eṣ-ṣeyd), surround the spot in which the game is found.

"On the eastern frontiers of Syria," says Burckhardt, "are several places allotted for the hunting of gazelles: these places are called 'masiade' [perhaps more properly, 'maṣyedehs']. An open space in the plain, of about one mile and a half square, is enclosed on three sides by a wall of loose stones, too high for the gazelles to leap over. In different parts of this wall, gaps are purposely left, and near each gap a deep ditch is made on the outside. The enclosed space is situated near some rivulet or spring to which in summer the gazelles resort. When the hunting is to begin, many peasants assemble, and watch till they see a herd of gazelles advancing from a distance towards the enclosure, into which they drive them: the gazelles, frightened by the shouts of these people and the discharge of fire-arms, endeavour to leap over the wall, but can only effect this at the gaps, where they fall into the ditch outside, and are easily taken, sometimes by hundreds. The chief of the herd always leaps first: the others follow him one by one. The gazelles thus taken are immediately killed, and their flesh is sold to the Arabs and neighbouring Felláḥs."[1] Hunting the wild ass is among the most difficult sports of the Arabs and Persians.

[1] Notes on the Bedouins and Wahábys, i. 220, ff.

CHAPTER VIII.

CHILDHOOD AND EDUCATION.

In few cases are the Mohammadans so much fettered by the directions of their Prophet and other religious instructors as in the rearing and education of their children. In matters of the most trivial nature, religious precedents direct their management of the young. One of the first duties is to wrap the new-born child in clean white linen, or in linen of some other colour, but not yellow. After this some person (not a female) should pronounce the adán[1] in the ear of the infant, because the Prophet did so in the ear of El-Ḥasan when Fáṭimeh gave birth to him; or he should pronounce the adán in the right ear, and the iḳámeh (which is nearly the same) in the left.[2]

[1] The call to prayer which is chanted from the mádinehs (or minarets) of the mosques. It is as follows:—"God is most great!" (four times). "I testify that there is no deity but God!" (twice). "I testify that Moḥammad is God's Apostle!" (twice). "Come to prayer!" (twice). "Come to security!" (twice). "God is most great!" (twice). "There is no deity but God!"

[2] Nuzhet el-Mutaämmil, section 9. The ikámeh differs from the adán in adding "The time for prayer is come" twice after "come to security."

It was formerly a custom of many of the Arabs, and perhaps is still among some, for the father to give a feast to his friends on seven successive days after the birth of a son; but that of a daughter was observed with less rejoicing. The general modern custom is to give an entertainment only on the seventh day, which is called Yóm es-Subooạ.

On this occasion, in the families of the higher classes, professional female singers are hired to entertain a party of ladies, friends of the infant's mother, who visit her on this occasion, in the ḥareem; or a concert of instrumental music, or a recitation of the whole of the Ḳur-án, is performed below by men. The mother, attended by the midwife, being seated in a chair which is the property of the latter, the child is brought, wrapped in a handsome shawl or something costly; and, to accustom it to noise, that it may not be frightened afterwards by the music and other sounds of mirth, one of the women takes a brass mortar and strikes it repeatedly with the pestle, as if pounding. After this, the child is put into a sieve and shaken, it being supposed that this operation is beneficial to its stomach. Next, it is carried through all the apartments of the ḥareem, accompanied by several women or girls, each of whom bears a number of wax candles, sometimes of various colours, cut in two, lighted, and stuck into small lumps of paste of ḥennà, upon a small round tray. At the same time the midwife, or another female, sprinkles upon the floor of each room a mixture of salt with seed of the fennel-flower, or salt alone, which has been placed during the preceding night at the infant's head; saying as she does this, "The salt be in the eye of the person who doth not bless the Prophet!" or, "The foul salt be in the eye of the envier!" This ceremony of the sprinkling of salt is considered a preservative for the child and mother from the evil eye; and each person present should say, "O God, bless our lord Moḥammad!" The child, wrapped up and placed on a fine mattress, which is sometimes laid on a silver tray, is shewn to each of the women present, who looks at its face, says, "O God, bless our lord Moḥammad! God give thee long life!" etc., and usually puts an embroidered handkerchief, with a gold coin (if pretty or old, the more esteemed) tied up in one of the corners, on the child's head, or by its side. This giving of handkerchiefs and gold is considered as imposing a debt, to be repaid by the mother, if the donor should give her the same occasion; or as the discharge of a debt for a similar offering. The coins are generally used for some years to decorate the head-dress of the child. After these presents for the child, others are given for the midwife. During the night before the seventh-day's festivity, a water-bottle full of water (a dórak in the case of a boy, and a ḳulleh[1]

[1] The dórak has a long narrow neck, the ḳulleh a short wide one.

in that of a girl), with an embroidered handkerchief tied round the neck, is placed at the child's head while it sleeps. This, with the water it contains, the midwife takes and puts upon a tray and presents it to each of the women; who put presents of money for her into the tray. In the evening, the husband generally entertains a party of his friends.[1]

On this day, or on the fourteenth, twenty-first, twenty-eighth, or thirty-fifth day after the birth, several religious ceremonies are required to be performed; but they are most approved if observed on the seventh day. One of these is the naming. I believe, however, that it is a more common custom to give the name almost immediately after the birth, or about three hours after. Astrologers were often consulted on this occasion; but the following directions are given on higher authority, and are generally followed.—"The father should give his son a good name, . . . not a name of self-praise, as Rasheed [Orthodox], Emeen [Faithful], etc. . . . The Prophet said, 'The names most approved by God are 'Abd-Allah [Servant of God] and 'Abd-Er-Raḥmán [Servant of the Compassionate], and such like.' He also said, 'Give my name, but do not distinguish by my surname of relationship:' but this precept, they say, respects his own lifetime, . . . because he was addressed, 'O Abu-l-Ḳásim!' and now it is not disapproved; but some

[1] See Modern Egyptians, chap. xiv.

disapprove of uniting the name and surname, so as to call a person Moḥammad and Abu-l-Ḳásim. And if a son be called by the name of a prophet it is not allowable to abuse or vilify him, unless the person so named be facing his reproacher, who should say, 'Thou' [without mentioning his name]: and a child named Moḥammad or Aḥmad should be [especially] honoured. . . . The Prophet said, 'There is no people holding a consultation at which there is present one whose name is Moḥammad or Aḥmad, but God blesseth all that assembly:' and again he said, 'Whoever nameth his child by my name, or by that of any of my children or my companions, from affection to me or to them, God (whose name be exalted) will give him in Paradise what eye hath not seen nor ear heard.' And a son should not be named King of kings, or Lord of lords; nor should a man take a surname of relationship from the name of the eldest of his children; nor take any such surname before a child is born to him."[1] The custom of naming children after prophets, or after relations or companions of Moḥammad, is very common. No ceremony is observed on account of the naming.

On the same day, however, two practices which I am about to mention are prescribed to be observed; though, as far as my observations and inquiries allow me to judge, they are generally neglected by the modern Muslims. The first of these is a sacrifice.

[1] Nuzhet el-Mutaämmil, section 9.

The victim is called 'aḳeeḳah. It should be a ram or goat; or two such animals should be sacrificed for a son, and one for a daughter. This rite is regarded by Ibn-Ḥambal as absolutely obligatory: he said, "If a father sacrifice not for his son, and he [the son] die, that son will not intercede for him on the day of judgment." The founders of the three other principal sects regard it in different and less important lights, though Moḥammad slew an 'aḳeeḳah for himself after his prophetic mission. The person should say, on slaying the victim, "O God, verily this 'aḳeeḳah is a ransom for my son such a one; its blood for his blood, and its flesh for his flesh, and its bone for his bone, and its skin for his skin, and its hair for his hair. O God, make it a ransom for my son from hell fire." A bone of the victim should not be broken.[1] The midwife should receive a leg of it. It should be cooked without previously cutting off any portion of it; and part of it should be given in alms.

After this should be performed the other ceremony above alluded to, which is this:—It is a sunneh ordinance, incumbent on the father, to shave or cause to be shaved the head of the child, and to give in alms to the poor the weight of the hair in gold or silver. This should also be done for a proselyte.[2] On the subsequent occasions of shaving the head of a

[1] Compare Exodus xiii. 13; and xii. 46.

[2] Nuzhet el-Mutaämmil, section 9; and Mishkát el-Maṣábeeḥ, ii. 315, f.

male child (for the head of the male is frequently shaven), a tuft of hair is generally left on the crown, and commonly for several years another also over the forehead.

Circumcision is most approved if performed on the same day; [1] but the observance of this rite is generally delayed until the child has attained the age of five or six years, and sometimes several years later. (See p. 200).

The Muslims regard a child as a trust committed by God to its parents, who, they hold, are responsible for the manner in which they bring it up, and will be examined on this subject on the day of judgment. But they further venture to say, that "the first who will lay hold of a man on the day of judgment will be his wife and children, who [if he have been deficient in his duty to them] will present themselves before God, and say, 'O our Lord, take for us our due from him; for he taught us not that of which we were ignorant, and he fed us with forbidden food, and we knew not:' and their due will be taken from him." [2] By this is meant, that a certain proportion of the good works which the man may have done, and his children and wife neglected, will be set down to their account: or that a similar proportion of their evil works will be transferred to *his* account.

The mother is enjoined by the law to give suck to

[1] Nuzhet el-Mutaämmil, section 9. [2] Ibid.

her child two full years, unless she have her husband's consent to shorten the period, or to employ another nurse. "For suckling the child, a virtuous woman, who eateth only what is lawful, should be chosen; for the unlawful [food] will manifest its evil in the child; as the Prophet . . . said, 'Giving suck altereth the tempers.' But it is recommended by the Sunneh that the mother herself suckle the child; for it is said in a tradition, 'There is nothing better for a child than its mother's milk.' 'If thou wouldst try,' it is added, 'whether the child be of an ingenuous disposition in its infancy or not, order a woman who is not its mother to suckle it after its mother has done so: and if it drink of the milk of the woman who is not its mother, it is not of an ingenuous disposition.'"[1]

Children, being regarded by Muslim parents as enviable blessings, are to them objects of the most anxious solicitude. To guard them from the supposed influence of the envious or evil eye, they have recourse to various expedients. When they are taken abroad, they are usually clad in a most slovenly manner, and left unwashed, or even purposely smeared with dirt; and as a further precaution a fantastic cap is often put upon the child's head, or its head-dress is decorated with one or more coins, a feather, a gay tassel, or a written charm or two sewed up in leather or encased in gold or silver, or some other appendage to attract the

[1] Nuzhet el-Mutaämmil, l.l.

eye, that so the infant itself may pass unnoticed. If a person express his admiration of another's child otherwise than by some pious ejaculation, as for instance by praising its Creator (with the exclamation of "Subḥána-lláh!" or Má sháa-lláh!" etc.) or invoking a blessing on the Prophet, he fills the mind of the parent with apprehension; and recourse is had to some superstitious ceremony to counteract the dreaded influence of his envious glance. The children of the poor from their unattractive appearance are less exposed to this imaginary danger: they generally have little or no clothing and are extremely dirty. It is partly with the view of protecting them from the evil eye that those of the rich are so long confined to the ḥareem: there they are petted and pampered for several years, at least until they are of age to go to school; but most of them are instructed at home.

The children of the Muslims are taught to show to their fathers a degree of respect which might be deemed incompatible with the existence of a tender mutual affection; but I believe that this is not the case. The child greets the father in the morning by kissing his hand, and then usually stands before him in a respectful attitude, with the left hand covered by the right, to receive any order or to await his permission to depart; but after the respectful kiss, is often taken on the lap. After the period of infancy, the well-bred son seldom sits in the presence of his father; but during that period he is generally allowed much familiarity. A Syrian merchant, who was one of my near neighbours in Cairo, had a child of exquisite beauty, commonly supposed to be his daughter, whom, though he was a most bigoted Muslim, he daily took with him from his private house to his shop. The child followed him, seated upon an ass before a black slave, and until about six years old was dressed like most young ladies, but without a face-veil. The father then thinking that the appearance of taking about with him a daughter of that age was scandalous, dressed his pet as a boy, and told his friends that the female attire had been employed as a protection against the evil eye, girls being less coveted than boys. This indeed is sometimes done, and it is possible that such might have been the case in this instance; but I was led to believe that it was not so. A year after, I left Cairo: while I remained there, I continued to see the child pass my house as before, but always in boy's clothing.

It is not surprising that the natives of Eastern countries, where a very trifling expense is required to rear the young, should be generally desirous of a numerous offspring. A motive of self-interest conduces forcibly to cherish this feeling in a wife; for she is commonly esteemed by her husband in proportion to her fruitfulness, and a man is seldom willing to divorce a wife, or to sell a slave, who has borne him a child. A similar feeling also induces in both parents a desire to obtain offspring, and renders them at the same time resigned to the loss of such of their children as die in tender age. This feeling arises from their belief of certain services, of greater moment than the richest blessings this world can bestow, which children who die in infancy are to render to their parents.

The Prophet is related to have said, "The infant children [of the Muslims] shall assemble at the scene of judgment on the day of the general resurrection, when all creatures shall appear for the reckoning, and it will be said to the angels, 'Go ye with these into Paradise:' and they will halt at the gate of Paradise, and it will be said to them, 'Welcome to the offspring of the Muslims! enter ye Paradise: there is no reckoning to be made with you:' and they will reply, 'Yea, and our fathers and our mothers:' but the guardians of Paradise will say, 'Verily your fathers and your mothers are not with you because they have committed faults and sins for which they must be reckoned with and inquired of.' Then they will shriek and cry at the gate of Paradise with a great cry; and God (whose name be exalted, and who is all-knowing respecting them) will say, 'What is this cry?' It will be answered, 'O our Lord, the children of the Muslims say, We will not enter Paradise but with our fathers and our mothers.' Whereupon God (whose name be exalted) will say, 'Pass among them all, and take the hands of your parents, and introduce them into Paradise.'" The children who are to have this power are such as are born of believers, and die without having attained to the knowledge of sin; and according to one tradition, one such child will introduce his two parents into Paradise. Such infants only are to enter Paradise; for of the children who die in infancy, those of believers alone are they who would believe if they grew to years of discretion. On the same authority it is said, "When a child of the servant [of God] dies, God (whose name be exalted) saith to the angels, 'Have ye taken the child of my servant?' They answer, 'Yea.' He saith, 'Have ye taken the child of his heart?' They reply, 'Yea.' He asketh them, 'What did my servant say?' They answer, 'He praised thee, and said, Verily to God we belong, and verily unto Him we return!' Then God will say, 'Build for my servant a house in Paradise, and name it the House of Praise.'"

To these traditions, which I find related as proofs of the advantages of marriage, the following anecdote, which is of a similar nature, is added. A certain man who would not take a wife awoke one day from his sleep, and demanded to be married, saying as his reason, "I dreamed that the resurrection had taken place, and that I was among the beings collected at the scene of judgment, but was suffering a thirst that stopped up the passage of my stomach;

and lo, there were youths passing through the assembly, having in their hands ewers of silver, and cups of gold, and giving drink to one person after another; so I stretched forth my hand to one of them, and said, 'Give me to drink; for thirst overpowereth me;' but they answered, 'Thou hast no child among us; we give drink only to our fathers.' I asked them, 'Who are ye?' They replied, 'We are the deceased infant children of the Muslims.'"[1] Especial rewards in heaven are promised to mothers. "When a woman conceives by her husband," said the Prophet, "she is called in heaven a martyr [*i.e.* she is ranked, as a martyr in dignity]; and her labour in childbed and her care for her children protect her from hell fire."[2]

"When the child begins to speak, the father should teach him first the kelimeh [or profession of faith], 'There is no deity but God: [Moḥammad is God's apostle]'—he should dictate this to him seven times. Then he should instruct him to say, 'Wherefore exalted be God, the King, the Truth! There is no deity but He, the Lord of the honourable throne."[3] He should teach him also the Throne-verse,[4] and the closing words of the Ḥashr, 'He is God, beside whom there is no deity, the King, the Holy,'" etc.[5]

As soon as a son is old enough, his father should

[1] Nuzhet el-Mutaämmil, section 2. [2] Idem., section 7.

[3] Ḳur-án, xxiii. 117.

[4] "God! there is no deity but He," etc., Ḳur. ii. 256.

[5] Nuzhet el-Mutaämmil, section 9.

teach him the most important rules of decent behaviour: placing some food before him, he should order him to take it with the right hand (the left being employed for unclean purposes), and to say, on commencing, "In the name of God;" to eat what is next to him, and not to hurry or spill any of the food upon his person or dress. He should teach him that it is disgusting to eat much. He should particularly condemn to him the love of gold and silver, and caution him against covetousness as he would against serpents and scorpions; and forbid his spitting in an assembly and every similar breach of good manners, from talking much, turning his back upon another, standing in an indolent attitude, and speaking ill of any person to another. He should keep him from bad companions, teach him the Ḳur-án and all requisite divine and prophetic ordinances, and instruct him in the arts of swimming and archery, and in some virtuous trade; for trade is a security from poverty. He should also command him to endure patiently the chastisements of his teacher. In one tradition it is said, "When a boy attains the age of six years he should be disciplined, and when he attains to nine years he should be put in a separate bed, and when he attains to ten years he should be beaten for [neglecting] prayer:" and in another tradition, "Order your children to pray at seven [years], and beat them for [neglecting] it at ten, and put them in separate beds."[1]

[1] Nuzhet el-Mutaämmil, section 9.

Circumcision is generally performed before the boy is submitted to the instruction of the schoolmaster.[1] Previously to the performance of this rite, he is, if belonging to the higher or middle rank of society, usually paraded about the neighbourhood of his parents' dwelling, gaily attired, chiefly with female habits and ornaments, but with a boy's turban on his head, mounted on a horse, preceded by musicians, and followed by a group of his female relations and friends. This ceremony is observed by the great with much pomp and with sumptuous feasts. El-Jabartee mentions a fête celebrated on the occasion of the circumcision of a son of the Ḳáḍee of Cairo, in the year of the Flight 1179 (A. D. 1766), when the grandees and chief merchants and 'ulamà of the city sent him such abundance of presents that the magazines of his mansion were filled with rice and butter and honey and sugar; the great hall, with coffee; and the middle of the court, with fire-wood: the public were amused for many days by players and performers of various kinds; and when the youth was paraded through the streets he was attended by numerous memlooks with their richly caparisoned horses and splendid arms and armour and military band, and by a number of other youths,

[1] An analogous custom is mentioned in a note appended to the account of circumcision in chap. ii. of my work on the Modern Egyptians.

who, out of compliment to him, were afterwards circumcised with him. This last custom is usual on such occasions; and so also is the sending of presents, such as those above mentioned, by friends, acquaintances, and tradespeople. At a fête of this kind, when the Khaleefeh El-Muḳtedir circumcised five of his sons, the money that was scattered in presents amounted to six hundred thousand pieces of gold, or about £300,000. Many orphans were also circumcised on the same day, and were presented with clothes and pieces of gold.[1] The Khaleefeh above mentioned was famous for his magnificence, a proof of which I have given before (p. 122 ff.). At the more approved entertainments which are given in celebration of a circumcision, a recital of the whole of the Ḳur-án, or a zikr, is performed: at some others, male or female public dancers perform in the court of the house or in the street before the door.

Few of the children of the Arabs receive much instruction in literature, and still fewer are taught even the rudiments of any of the higher sciences; but there are numerous schools in their towns, and one at least in almost every moderately large village. The former are mostly attached to mosques and other public buildings, and, together with those buildings, are endowed by princes or other men of rank, or wealthy tradesmen. In these the children are instructed either gratis or

[1] Mir-át ez-Zemán, events of the year 302.

for a very trifling weekly payment, which all parents save those in indigent circumstances can easily afford. The schoolmaster generally teaches nothing more than to read, and to recite by heart the whole of the Ḳur-án. After committing to memory the first chapter of the sacred volume, the boy learns the rest in the inverse order of their arrangement, as they generally decrease in length (the longest coming first, and the shortest at the end). Writing and arithmetic are usually taught by another master; and grammar, rhetoric, versification, logic, the interpretation of the Ḳur-án, and the whole system of religion and law, with all other knowledge deemed useful, which seldom includes the mere elements of mathematics, are attained by studying at a collegiate mosque, and at no expense; for the professors receive no pay either from the students, who are mostly of the poorer classes, or from the funds of the mosque.

The wealthy often employ for their sons a private tutor; and when he has taught them to read, and to recite the Ḳur-án, engage for them a writing-master, and then send them to the college. But among this class, polite literature is more considered than any other branch of knowledge, after religion. Such an acquaintance with the works of some of their favourite poets as enables a man to quote them occasionally in company, is regarded by the Arabs as essential to a son who is to mix in good society; and to this acquirement is often added some skill in the art of versification, which is rendered peculiarly easy by the copiousness of the Arabic language and by its system of inflexion. These characteristics of their noble tongue (which are remarkably exhibited by the custom, common among the Arabs, of preserving the same rhyme throughout a whole poem), while on the one hand they have given an admirable freedom to the compositions of men of true poetic genius, have on the other hand mainly contributed to the degradation of Arabic poetry. To an Arab of some little learning it is almost as easy to speak in verse as in prose; and hence he often intersperses his prose writings, and not unfrequently his conversation, with indifferent verses, of which the chief merit generally consists in puns or in an ingenious use of several words nearly the same in sound but differing in sense. This custom is frequently exemplified in the "Thousand and One Nights," where a person suddenly changes the style of his speech from prose to verse, and then reverts to the former.

One more duty of a father to a son I should here mention: it is to procure for him a wife as soon as he has arrived at a proper age. This age is decided by some to be twenty years, though many young men marry at an earlier period. It is said, "When a son has attained the age of twenty years, his father, if able, should marry him, and then take his hand and say, 'I have disciplined thee and taught thee and married thee: I now seek refuge with God from thy mischief in the present world and the next.'" To enforce this duty, the following tradition is urged: "When a son becomes adult and his father does not marry him and yet is able to do so, if the youth do wrong in consequence, the sin of it is between the two"—or, as in another report,—"on the father."[1] The same is held to be the case with respect to a daughter who has attained the age of twelve years.

The female children of the Arabs are seldom taught even to read. Though they are admissible at the daily schools in which the boys are instructed, very few parents allow them the benefit of this privilege; preferring, if they give them any instruction of a literary kind, to employ a sheykhah (or learned woman) to teach them at home. She instructs them in the forms of prayer and teaches them to repeat by heart a few chapters of the Ḳur-án, very rarely the whole book. Parents are indeed recommended to withhold from their daughters some portions of the Ḳur-án; to "teach them the Soorat ed-Noor [or 24th chapter], and keep from them the Soorat Yoosuf [12th chapter]; on account of the story of Zeleekhà and Yoosuf in the latter, and the prohibitions and threats and mention of punishments contained in the former."[2]

Needle-work is not so rarely, but yet not generally,

[1] Nuzhet el-Mutaämmil, section 9, and Misḳát el-Maṣábeeḥ, ii. 86.
[2] Nuzhet el-Mutäammil, section 6.

taught to Arab girls, the spindle frequently employs those of the poorer classes, and some of them learn to weave. The daughters of persons of the middle and higher ranks are often instructed in the art of embroidery and in other ornamental work, which are taught in schools and in private houses. Singing and playing upon the lute, which were formerly not uncommon female accomplishments among the wealthy Arabs, are now almost exclusively confined, like dancing, to professional performers and a few of the slaves in the ḥareems of the great: it is very seldom now that any musical instrument is seen in the hand of an Arab lady except a kind of drum called darabukkeh and a ṭár (or tambourine), which are found in many ḥareems, and are beaten with the fingers.[1] Some care, however, is bestowed by the ladies in teaching their daughters what they consider an elegant gait and carriage, as well as various alluring and voluptuous arts with which to increase the attachment of their future husbands.

I have heard Arabs confess that their nation possesses nine-tenths of the envy that exists among all mankind collectively; but I have not seen any written authority for this. Ibn-'Abbás assigns nine-tenths of the intrigue or artifice that exists in the world to the Copts, nine-tenths of the perfidy to the Jews, nine-tenths of the stupidity to the Maghrabees, nine-

[1] See Modern Egyptians, ch. xviii.

tenths of the hardness to the Turks, and nine-tenths of the bravery to the Arabs. According to Kaab El-Aḥbár, reason and sedition are most peculiar to Syria, plenty and degradation to Egypt, and misery and health to the Desert. In another account, faith and modesty are said to be most peculiar to El-Yemen, fortitude and sedition to Syria, magnificence or pride and hypocrisy to El-'Irák, wealth and degradation to Egypt, and poverty and misery to the Desert. Of women, it is said by Kaab El-Aḥbár, that the best in the world (excepting those of the tribe of Ḳureysh mentioned by the Prophet) are those of El-Baṣrah; and the worst in the world, those of Egypt.[1]

[1] El-Maḳreezee's Khiṭaṭ, and El-Isḥáḳee.

CHAPTER IX.

WOMEN.

THAT sensual passion is very prevalent among the Arabs cannot be doubted; but I think it unjust to suppose them generally incapable of a purer feeling, worthy, if constancy be a sufficient test, of being termed true love. That they are not so, appears evident to almost every person who mixes with them in familiar society; for such a person must have opportunities of being acquainted with many Arabs sincerely attached to wives whose personal charms have long vanished, and who have neither wealth nor influence of their own, nor wealthy or influential relations, to induce their husbands to refrain from divorcing them. It very often happens, too, that an Arab is sincerely attached to a wife possessed, even in the best portion of her age, of few charms, and that the lasting favourite among two or more wives is not the most handsome. This opinion, I am sorry to observe, is at variance, as far as the Arabs of the *towns* are concerned, with that entertained by one of the most intelligent and experienced of modern travellers who long resided among this people,—the justly celebrated Burckhardt:[1] but it is confirmed by numerous facts related by respectable Arab authors (and therefore not regarded by them as of an incredible nature), as well as by cases which have fallen under my own observation. The tale of Leylà and Mejnoon, the Juliet and Romeo of Arabia, is too well known to be here repeated; but among many other anecdotes of strong and constant love, the following may be inserted.

The Khaleefeh Yezeed, the son of 'Abd-El-Melik, had two female slaves, one of whom was named

[1] I may suffer in public estimation for my differing in opinion from this accomplished traveller and most estimable man; but I cannot, on that account, abstain from the expression of my dissent. Our difference, I think, may be thus explained. He conformed, in a great degree, to the habits of the Arabs; but not to such an extent as I consider necessary to obtain from them that confidence in his sympathy which would induce them to lay open to him their character; and when a man is often treated with coldness and reserve, I doubt whether the people from whom he experiences such treatment can be judged by him with strict impartiality. To be received on terms of equality by Arabs of the more polished classes, an undeviating observance of their code of etiquette is absolutely indispensable: but Burckhardt, I have been assured, often violated this code by practices harmless enough to our notions and probably also in the opinion of the Arabs of the Desert, but extremely offensive to the people who enjoyed the least share of his esteem: his most intimate acquaintances in Cairo generally refused, in speaking of him, to designate him by the title of "sheykh" which he had adopted; and yet the heaviest charge that I heard brought against him was his frequent habit of *whistling!*—This fact has been mentioned, as corroborating an observation of the same kind, by Mr. Urquhart ("Spirit of the East," i. 417, 418), all of whose opinions relating to the East, expressed in that work, and especially those regarding the characteristics of the Eastern *mind,* are entitled to the highest respect.

Habbábeh and the other, Selámeh, to the former of whom he was most ardently attached: he had purchased her for a hundred thousand dirhems, and the other for ten thousand. In their company he sometimes shut himself up for three months together, utterly neglecting the affairs of his people. At length, being reproved for this conduct by his brother Meslemeh, he promised to return to his duty: but the two slaves diverted him from his purpose; and on the following morning excited by their songs and caresses and by wine, he became frantic with pleasure, and danced and sang like a madman, till a fatal accident put a stop to his joy:—Ḥabbábeh, eating a pomegranate, was choked by one of the grains, and immediately died.

The grief of Yezeed was so poignant that he would not quit the corpse, but continued to kiss and fondle it, until it became corrupt. Being then admonished by his attendants that proper respect required its burial, he consented to commit it to the earth. After five days, however, his desire to behold again the object of his love induced him to open the grave, and though the corpse had become hideous he declared that it was lovely as ever in his eyes. At the earnest request of Meslemeh, he ordered the grave to be closed again, but he was unable to exist when deprived of the sight of the remains of her who was at the same time his slave and his mistress: he threw himself upon his bed, speechless, and after lingering seventeen nights, expired and was buried by the side of Ḥabbábeh. "May God," says the narrator, "have mercy on them both!"[1]

In the same work from which the above is taken, it is related that Hároon Er-Rasheed, visiting Suleymán the son of Aboo-Jaạfar, one of his chief officers, saw with him a female slave, named Da'eefeh, of excessive beauty, and being smitten by her charms demanded her as a present. His request was granted; but Suleymán, from grief at the loss of his mistress, fell sick; and during his illness was heard to exclaim,—

> "I appeal unto God against the affliction which He hath sent upon me through the Khaleefeh.
>
> "The world heareth of his justice; but he is a tyrant in the affair of Ḍa'eefeh.[2]
>
> "Love of her is fixed in my heart as ink upon the surface of paper."

Er-Rasheed, being informed of his complaint, restored to him his mistress, and with her his peace of mind. This anecdote is given as a proof of strong love; but perhaps may not be thought much to the purpose. The following, from the same work, is more apt.

During the hottest hour of an excessively sultry day, the Khaleefeh Mo'áwiyeh the son of Aboo-Sufyán

[1] Kitáb el-'Onwán fee Mekáïd en-Niswán, a work on the stratagems of women (MS.).

[2] This word slightly varied (changed to Ḍa'eefih) bears another meaning, namely, "his weak one:" the final vowel being suppressed by the rule of waḳf.

was sitting in a chamber which was open on each side to allow free passage to the air, when he beheld a barefooted Bedawee approaching him. Wondering what could induce this man to brave the scorching heat, he declared to his attendants that if he were come to demand of him any favour or aid or act of justice, his request should be granted. The Bedawee addressed him in verse with a pathetic appeal for justice against the tyranny of Marwán the son of El-Ḥakam (afterwards Khaleefeh, Mo'áwiyeh's fourth successor), by whom he had been forcibly deprived of his beloved wife Soạdà. The Khaleefeh requiring a more particular account of his case, he related the following facts. He had a wife, the daughter of his paternal uncle, excessively beloved by him, and possessed a number of camels, which enabled him to live in comfort; but a year of terrible drought deprived him of his property and reduced him to utter want: his friends deserted him, and his wife was taken away from him by her father. To seek redress he repaired to Marwán, the Governor of his district, at El-Medeeneh, who, having summoned the father of his wife, and herself, was so smitten by the beauty of the woman that he determined to obtain her for himself in marriage. To accomplish this, he threw the husband into prison, and offered the father of the woman a thousand deenárs and ten thousand dirhems for his consent to his marriage with her, promising to compel her actual husband to divorce her; and this latter object, having obtained the father's approval, he gained by severely torturing the unfortunate Bedawee. It would have been vain for the woman to attempt resistance; and so she became the wife of Marwán.

The oppressed Bedawee, having related these circumstances, fell down in a swoon, and lay on the floor senseless, coiled up like a dead snake. As soon as he recovered, the Khaleefeh wrote a poetical epistle to Marwán, severely reproaching him for his baseness, and commanding him, on pain of death, to divorce the woman and send her with his messenger. She was accordingly divorced and sent, with an answer composed in the same measure and rhyme, assuring the Khaleefeh that the sight of Soạdà would convince him that her charms were irresistible; and this proved too true. Mo'áwiyeh himself no sooner saw her than he coveted her, and offered to give the Bedawee, if he would resign her to him, three virgins from among his female slaves, together with a thousand deenárs and an ample annual pension. The Bedawee shrieked with dismay, as though he had received his death-blow, and indignantly rejected the offer. The Khaleefeh then said to him, "Thou confessest that thou hast divorced her, and Marwán has married her and acknowledged that he has divorced her: we will therefore give her her choice: if she desire any other than thee as her husband we will marry her to him, and if she prefer thee we will restore her to thee." She, however, had the merit to prefer the destitute Bedawee, and the Khaleefeh gave her up to him, with a present of ten thousand dirhems.

Numerous instances of unreasonable love are recorded in the writings of Arabs. It is related that a man fell in love with a lady from seeing the impression of her hand upon a wall; and, being unable to win her, died. Many men are said to have conceived a violent passion for damsels seen in dreams; others, again, to have been affected thus merely by the ear. An author relates his having been acquainted with an accomplished schoolmaster who lost his heart from hearing a man sing the praises of a woman named Umm-'Amr, and two days after shut himself up in his house to mourn for her death, in consequence of his hearing the same man sing,—

> "The ass went away with Umm-'Amr; and she returned not, nor did the ass return." [1]

The reader should have some idea of the qualifications or charms which the Arabs in general consider requisite to the perfection of female beauty. He must not imagine that excessive fatness is one of these characteristics, though it is said to be esteemed a chief essential to beauty throughout the greater part

[1] Kitáb el-'Onwán.

of Northern Africa: on the contrary, the maiden whose loveliness inspires the most impassioned expressions in Arabic poesy and prose is celebrated for her slender figure,—she is like the cane among plants, and is elegant as a twig of the oriental willow. Her face is like the full moon, presenting the strongest contrast to the colour of her hair, which (to preserve the nature of the simile just employed) is of the deepest hue of night, and falls to the middle of her back. A rosy blush overspreads the centre of each cheek; and a mole is considered an additional charm. The Arabs, indeed, are particularly extravagant in their admiration of this natural beauty-spot; which, according to its place, is compared to a drop of ambergris upon a dish of alabaster or upon the surface of a ruby. The Anacreon of Persia affected to prize the mole upon the cheek of his beloved above the cities of Samarḳand and Bukhárà.

The eyes of the Arab beauty are intensely black,[1] large, and long, of the form of an almond: they are full of brilliancy, but this is softened by a lid slightly depressed and by long silken lashes, giving a tender and languid expression that is full of enchantment and scarcely to be improved by the adventitious aid of the black border of koḥl; for this the lovely maiden

[1] The Arabs in general entertain a prejudice against blue eyes; a prejudice said to have arisen from the great number of blue-eyed persons among certain of their northern enemies.

adds rather for the sake of fashion than necessity, having what the Arabs term natural koḥl. The eyebrows are thin and arched; the forehead is wide, and fair as ivory; the nose, straight; the mouth, small; the lips of a brilliant red; and the teeth, "like pearls set in coral." The forms of the bosom are compared to two pomegranates; the waist is slender; the hips are wide and large; the feet and hands, small; the fingers, tapering, and their extremities dyed with the deep orange-red tint imparted by the leaves of the ḥennà. The maid in whom these charms are combined exhibits a lively image of "the rosy-fingered Aurora:" her lover knows neither night nor sleep in her presence, and the constellations of heaven are no longer seen by him when she approaches. The most bewitching age is between fourteen and seventeen years; for then the forms of womanhood are generally developed in their greatest beauty; but many a maiden in her twelfth year possesses charms sufficient to fascinate every man who beholds her.

The reader may perhaps desire a more minute analysis of Arabian beauty. The following is the most complete that I can offer him.—"Four things in a woman should be *black*,—the hair of the head, the eyebrows, the eyelashes, and the dark part of the eyes: four *white*,—the complexion of the skin, the white of the eyes, the teeth, and the legs: four *red*,—the tongue, the lips, the middle of the cheeks, and the gums: four *round,*—the head, the neck, the forearms, and the ankles: four *long,*—the back, the fingers, the arms, and the legs:[1] four *wide,*—the forehead, the eyes, the bosom, and the hips: four *fine,*—the eyebrows, the nose, the lips, and the fingers: four *thick,*—the lower part of the back, the thighs, the calves of the legs, and the knees: four *small,*—the ears, the breasts, the hands, and the feet."[2]

Arab ladies are extremely fond of full and long hair; and, however amply endowed with this natural ornament, to add to its effect they have recourse to art. But the Prophet, abhorring all false attractions that might at first deceive a husband and then disappoint him, "cursed the woman who joined her own hair to that of another, or that of another to her own, without her husband's permission: if she do it, therefore, with his permission, it is not prohibited, unless she so make use of human hair; for this is absolutely forbidden."[3] Hence the Arab women prefer strings of silk to add to their hair.[4] Over the forehead, the hair is cut rather

[1] In another analysis of the same kind, it is said that four should be *short,*—the hands, the feet, the tongue, and the teeth—but this is metaphorically speaking; the meaning is, that these members should be kept within their proper bounds. (Kitáb el-'Onwan.)

[2] An unnamed author quoted by El-Is-hákee, in his account of the 'Abbásee Khaleefeh El-Mutawekkil.

[3] Kitáb el-'Onwán.

[4] By sending with a letter the silk strings of her hair, a lady testifies the most abject submission. The same meaning is conveyed in a more forcible manner by sending the hair itself. Thus when Cairo was besieged by the Franks in the year of the Flight 564 (A.D.

short; but two full locks hang down on each side of the face: these are often curled in ringlets, and sometimes plaited. The rest of the hair is arranged in plaits or braids which hang down the back. They are generally from eleven to twenty-five in number, but always of an uneven number: eleven is considered a scanty number, thirteen and fifteen are more common. Three times the number of black silk strings (three to each plait of hair, and each three united at the top), from sixteen to eighteen inches in length, are braided with the hair for about a quarter of their length; or they are attached to a lace or band of black silk which is bound round the head, and in this case hang entirely separate from the plaits of hair. These strings, together with certain ornaments of gold, etc., composed what is termed the ṣafà. Along each string, except from the upper extremity to about a quarter or (at most) a third of its length, are generally attached nine or more little flat ornaments of gold, which are usually all of the same form. The most common form is oblong, round at the lower extremity and pointed at the upper, or the reverse. They are affixed (each by a little ring

1168), El-'Áḍid, the last Fáṭimee Khaleefeh, sent letters to Noor-ed-Deen Maḥmood, Sulṭán of Syria, imploring succour, and with them sent his women's hair to shew their subjection and his own. (Ibn Esh-Shihneh). [So too El-Makreezee, with a slight variation. It was in this siege that the old town now called erroneously Miṣr el-'aṭeeḳah was burnt by order of the Wezeer Sháwir, the conflagration lasting fifty-four days. (Khiṭaṭ, account of the ruin of El-Fusṭáṭ and reign of El-'Aḍid.) E. S. P.]

at its upper extremity) about an inch, or a little more, apart; but those of each string are purposely placed so as not exactly to correspond with those of the others. At the end of each string is a small gold tube, or a small polygonal gold bead, beneath which is most commonly suspended (by a little ring) a gold coin, a little more than half an inch in diameter. Such is the most general description of ṣafà; but some ladies substitute for the gold coin a fanciful ornament of the same metal, either simple, or with a pearl in the centre; or they suspend in the place of this a little tassel of pearls, or attach alternately pearls and emeralds to the bottom of the triple strings, and a pearl with each of the little ornaments of gold first mentioned. Coral beads are also sometimes attached in the same manner as these pearls. The ṣafà I think the prettiest, as well as most singular, of all the ornaments worn by Arab ladies. The glittering of the little ornaments of gold, and their chinking together as the wearer walks, have a peculiarly lively effect. A kind of crown—a circle of jewelled gold (the lower edge of which was straight, and the upper fancifully heightened to four or more points) surrounding the lower part of a dome-shaped cap with a jewel or some other ornament at the summit—was worn by many Arab ladies of high rank or great wealth, probably until about two centuries ago. Another kind of crown is now more generally worn, called a ḳurṣ. This is a round convex ornament, generally about five inches in diameter, composed of gold set with a profusion of diamonds, of open work, representing roses, leaves, etc. It is sewed upon the top of the ṭarboosh; and is worn by most of the ladies of Cairo, at least in full dress.[1]

The gait of Arab ladies is very remarkable: they incline the lower part of the body from side to side as they step, and with the hands raised to the level of the bosom they hold the edges of their outer covering. Their pace is slow, and they look not about them, but keep their eyes towards the ground in the direction to which they are going.

The wickedness of women is a subject upon which the stronger sex among the Arabs, with an affectation of superior virtue, often dwell in common conversation. That women are deficient in judgment or good sense is held as a fact not to be disputed even by themselves, as it rests on an assertion of the Prophet; but that they possess a superior degree of cunning is pronounced equally certain and notorious. Their general depravity is pronounced to be much greater than that of men. "I stood," said the Prophet, "at the gate of Paradise; and lo, most of its inmates were the poor: and I stood at the gate of Hell; and lo, most of its

[1] An engraving of a crown of this description, and another of one of a more common kind, may be seen in my work on the Modern Egyptians, Appendix A.

inmates were women."[1] In allusion to women, the Khaleefeh 'Omar said, "Consult them, and do the contrary of what they advise." But this is not to be done merely for the sake of opposing them, nor when other advice can be had. "It is desirable for a man," says a learned Imám, "before he enters upon any important undertaking, to consult ten intelligent persons among his particular friends; or if he have not more than five such friends, let him consult each of them twice; or if he have not more than one friend, he should consult him ten times, at ten different visits; if he have not one to consult, let him return to his wife, and consult her, and whatever she advises him to do, let him do the contrary: so shall he proceed rightly in his affair, and attain his object."[2] A truly virtuous wife is, of course, excepted in this rule: such a person is as much respected by Muslims as she is (at least, according to their own account) rarely met with by them. When woman was created, the Devil, we are told, was delighted, and said, "Thou art half of my host, and thou art the depository of my secret, and thou art my arrow, with which I shoot, and miss not."[3] What are termed by us affairs of gallantry were very common among the Pagan Arabs, and are scarcely less so among their Muslim posterity. They are, however,

[1] Kitáb el-'Onwán.

[2] El-Imám El-Jara'ee, in his book entitled "Shir'at el-Islám."

[3] Nuzhet el-Mutaämmil, section 2.

unfrequent among most tribes of Bedawees, and among the descendants of those tribes not long settled as cultivators. I remember being roused from the quiet that I generally enjoyed in an ancient tomb in which I resided at Thebes, by the cries of a young woman in the neighbourhood whom an Arab was severely beating for an impudent proposal she had made to him.

Marriage is regarded by the Muslims in general as a positive duty, and to neglect it without a sufficient excuse subjects a man to severe reproach. "When a servant [of God]," said the Prophet, "marries, verily he perfects half his religion."[1] He once asked a man, "Art thou married?" The man answered, "No." "And art thou," said he, "sound and healthy?" The answer was, "Yes." "Then," said Moḥammad, "thou art one of the brothers of the devils; for the most wicked among you are the unmarried, and the most vile among your dead are the unmarried; moreover the married are those who are acquitted of filthy conversation; and by Him in whose hand is my soul, the devil hath not a weapon more effective against the virtuous, both men and women, than the neglect of marriage."[2]

The number of wives whom a Muslim may have at the same time is four. He may marry free women, or

[1] Mishkát el-Maṣábeeḥ, ii. 79.

[2] Nuzhet el-Mutaämmil, section 1.

take concubine slaves, or have of both these classes. It is the opinion of most persons, I believe, among the more strictly religious, that a man may not have more than four women, whether they be wives alone, or concubine slaves alone, or of both classes together; but the practice of some of the companions of the Prophet, who cannot be accused of violating his precepts, affords a strong argument to the contrary. 'Alee, it is said, "was the most devout of the companions; but he had four wives and seventeen concubines besides, and married, after Fáṭimeh (may God be well pleased with her!), among all that he married and divorced, more than two hundred women: and sometimes he included four wives in one contract, and sometimes divorced four at one time, taking other four in their stead."[1] This may perhaps be an exaggerated statement, but it is certain that the custom of keeping an unlimited number of concubines was common among wealthy Muslims in the first century of the Mohammadan era, and has so continued. The famous author of the work above quoted urges the example of Solomon to prove that the possession of numerous concubines is not inconsistent with piety and good morals; not considering that God in the beginning made one male and but one female.

It has been mentioned that a Muslim may divorce his wife twice and each time take her back. This he

[1] Nuzhet el-Mutaämmil, section 1.

may do, even against her wish, during a fixed period, which cannot extend beyond three months, unless she be *enceinte*, in which latter case she must wait until the birth of her child before she will be at liberty to contract a new marriage. During this period the husband is obliged to maintain her. If he divorce her a third time, or by a triple sentence, he cannot take her again unless with her own consent and by a new contract and after another marriage has been consummated between her and another husband who also has divorced her.

It is not a common custom, especially among the middle ranks, for a Muslim to have more than one wife at the same time; but there are few of middle age who have not had several different wives at different periods, tempted to change by the facility of divorce.[1] The case of 'Alee has been mentioned above. Mugheyreh Ibn-Sheabeh married eighty women in the course of his life;[2] and several more remarkable instances of the love of change are recorded by Arab writers; the most extraordinary case

[1] By way of exception, however, on the woman's side, my sheykh [Moḥammad 'Eiyád Eṭ-Ṭantáwee] writes:—"Many persons reckon marrying a second time among the greatest of disgraceful actions. This opinion is most common in the country-towns and villages; and the relations of my mother are thus characterized, so that a woman of them, when her husband dieth while she is young, or divorceth her while she is young, passeth her life, however long it may be, in widowhood, and never marrieth a second time."

[2] Nuzhet el-Mutaämmil, section 1.

of this kind that I have met with was that of Moḥammad Ibn-Eṭ-Ṭeiyib, the dyer of Baghdád, who died in the year of the Flight 423, aged eighty-five years; of whom it is related on most respectable authority that he married more than nine hundred women![1] Supposing, therefore, that he married his first wife when he was fifteen years of age, he must have had, on the average, nearly thirteen wives *per annum*. The women, in general, cannot of course marry so many successive husbands, not only because a woman cannot have more than one husband at a time, but also because she cannot divorce her husband. There have been, however, many instances of Arab women who have married a surprising number of men in rapid succession. Among these may be mentioned Umm-Khárijeh, who gave occasion to a proverb on this subject. This woman, who was of the tribe of Bejeeleh, in El-Yemen, married upwards of forty husbands; and her son Khárijeh knew not who was his father. She used to contract a marriage in the quickest possible manner: a man saying to her, "Khiṭb" ("I ask"—in marriage), she replied "Nikḥ" ("I give"), and thus became his lawful wife. She had a very numerous progeny; several tribes originating from her.[2]

For the choice of a wife, a man generally relies on his mother or some other near female relation, or a pro-

[1] Mir-át ez-Zemán, events of the year above mentioned.

[2] Idem, Proverbs of the Arabs; and my Lexicon, *voce* "khaṭaba."

fessional female betrother (who is called "kháṭibeh"); for there are many women who perform this office for hire. The law allows him to see the face of the girl whom he proposes to marry, previously to his making the contract; but in the present day this liberty is seldom obtained, except among the lower orders. Unless in this case, a man is not allowed to see unveiled any woman but his own wife or slave, and those women to whom the law prohibits his uniting himself in marriage: nay, according to some he is not allowed to see his own niece unveiled, though he may not marry her.[1] It should be added that a slave may

[1] The izár, or eezár (for the word is written in two different ways), is a piece of drapery commonly worn by Arab women when they appear in public. It is about two yards or more in width (according to the height of the wearer), and three yards in length; one edge of it being drawn from behind, over the upper part of the head and forehead, and secured by a band sewed inside, the rest hangs down behind and on each side to the ground, or nearly so, and almost entirely envelops the person; the two ends being held so as nearly to meet in front. Thus it conceals every other part of the dress excepting a small portion of a very loose gown (which is another of the articles of walking or riding apparel), and the face-veil. It is now generally made of white calico, but a similar covering of black silk for the married, and of white silk for the unmarried, is now worn by women of the higher and middle classes, called a ḥabarah.

It appears that the kind of face-veil, called in Arabic ḳináạ is a piece of muslin, about a yard or more in length, and somewhat less in width, a portion of which is placed over the head, beneath the izár, the rest hanging down in front, to the waist, or thereabout, and entirely concealing the face. I have often seen Arab women, particularly those of the Wahhábees, wearing veils of this kind composed of printed muslin, completely concealing their features, yet of sufficiently loose fabric to admit of their seeing their way. But the

lawfully see the face of his own mistress; but this privilege is seldom granted in the present day to any slave but a eunuch. An infringement of the law above mentioned is held to be extremely sinful in both parties: "The curse of God," said the Prophet, "is on the seer and the seen:" yet it is very often disregarded in the case of women of the lower orders.

A man is forbidden, by the Ḳur-án[1] and the Sunneh, to marry his mother, or other ascendant; daughter, or other descendant; his sister, or half sister; the sister of his father or mother, or other ascendant; his niece, or any of her descendants; his foster-mother who has suckled him five times in the course of the first two years, or a woman related to him by milk in any of the degrees which would preclude his marriage with her if she were similarly related to him by consanguinity; the mother of his wife: the daughter of his wife, in certain conditions; his father's wife, and his son's wife; and to have at the same time two wives who are sisters, or aunt and

more common kind of Arab face-veil is a long strip of white muslin, or of a kind of black crape, covering the whole of the face excepting the eyes, and reaching nearly to the feet. It is suspended at the top by a narrow band, which passes up the forehead, and which is sewed, as are also the two upper corners of the veil, to a band that is tied round the head. This veil is called burḳo'. The black kind is often ornamented with gold coins, false pearls, etc., attached to the upper part. It is not so genteel as the white veil, unless for a lady in mourning.

[1] Chap. iv. 26, 27.

niece: he is forbidden also to marry his unemancipated slave, or another man's slave, if he has already a free wife; and to marry any woman but one of his own faith, or a Christian, or a Jewess. A Mohammadan woman, however, may only marry a man of her own faith. An unlawful liaison with any woman prevents a man from marrying any of her relations who would be forbidden to him if she were his wife.

A cousin (the daughter of a paternal uncle) is often chosen as a wife, on account of the tie of blood which is likely to attach her more strongly to her husband, or on account of an affection conceived in early years. Parity of rank is generally much regarded; and a man is often unable to obtain as his wife the daughter of one of a different profession or trade, unless an inferior; or a younger daughter when an elder remains unmarried. A girl is often married at the age of twelve years, and sometimes at ten, or even nine: the usual period is between twelve and sixteen years. At the age of thirteen or fourteen she may be a mother. The young men marry a few years later.

The most important requisite in a wife is religion. The Prophet said, "A virtuous wife is better than the world and all that it contains." "A virtuous wife," said Luḳmán, "is like a crown on the head of a king; and a wicked wife is like a heavy burden on the back of an old man." Among the other chief requisites are agreeableness of temper, beauty of form (undiminished by any defect or irregularity of features or members), moderation in the amount of dowry required, and good birth. It is said, "If thou marry not a virgin [which is most desirable], marry a divorced woman, and not a widow; for the divorced woman will respect thy words when thou sayest, 'If there were any good in thee thou hadst not been divorced;' whereas the widow will say, 'May God have mercy on such a one [her first husband]! he hath left me to one unsuited to me.'" But according to another selfish maxim, the woman most to be avoided is she who is divorced from a man by whom she has had a child; for her heart is with him, and she is an enemy to the man who marries her after.[1]

Modesty is a requisite upon which too much stress cannot be laid; but this, to an English reader, requires some explanation. 'Alee asked his wife Fáṭimeh, "Who is the best of women?" She answered, "She who sees not men, and whom they see not."[2] Modesty, therefore, in the opinion of the Muslims, is most eminently shewn by a woman's concealing her person, and restraining her eyes, from men. "The best rank of men [in a mosque]," said the Prophet, "is the front; and the best rank of women is the rear,"[3]—that is, those most distant from the men: but better than even these are the women who pray at home.[4] Fruit-

[1] Nuzhet el-Mutaämmil, section 4. [2] Idem, section 6.
[3] Mishkát el-Maṣábeeḥ, i. 229. [4] Idem, i. 223.

fulness is also a desirable qualification to be considered in the choice of a wife: "it may be known in maidens," said the Prophet, "from their relations; because, generally speaking, kindred are similar in disposition, etc."[1] Lastly, contentment is to be enumerated among the requisites. It is said, on the same authority, "Verily the best of women are those that are most content with little."[2] To obtain a contented and submissive wife, many men make their selection from among the classes inferior to them in rank. Others, with a similar view, prefer a slave in the place of a wife.

The consent of a young girl is not required: her father, or, if he be dead, her nearest adult male relation, or a guardian appointed by will or by the Ḳáḍee, acts as her wekeel or deputy, to effect the marriage-contract for her. If of age, she appoints her own deputy. A dowry is required to legalize the marriage; and the least dowry allowed by the law is ten dirhems,—about five shillings of our money. Moḥammad married certain of his wives for a dowry of ten dirhems and the household necessaries, which were a hand-mill to grind the corn, a water-jar, and a pillow of skin or leather stuffed with the fibres of the palm-tree (leef), but some he married for a dowry of five hundred dirhems.[3] With the increase of wealth and

[1] Mishkát el-Maṣábeeḥ, ii. 78. [2] Idem, ii. 79.
[3] Nuzhet el-Mutaämmil, section 4.

luxury, dowries have increased in amount; but to our ideas they are still trifling: a sum equivalent to about twenty pounds sterling being a common dowry among Arabs of the middle classes for a virgin, and half or a third or quarter of that sum for a divorced woman or a widow. Two thirds of the sum is usually paid before making the contract, and the remaining portion held in reserve to be paid to the woman in case of her divorce or in case of the husband's death. The father or guardian of a girl under age receives the former portion of her dowry; but it is considered as her property, and he generally expends it, with an additional sum from his own purse, in the purchase of necessary furniture, dress, etc., for her, which the husband can never take from her against her own wish.

The marriage-contract is generally, in the present day, merely verbal; but sometimes a certificate is written and sealed by the Ḳáḍee. The most approved or propitious period for this act is the month of Showwál: the most unpropitious, Moḥarram. The only persons whose presence is required to perform it are the bridegroom (or his deputy), the bride's deputy (who is the betrother), two male witnesses, if such can be easily procured, and the Ḳáḍee or a schoolmaster or some other person to recite a khuṭbeh, which consists of a few words in praise of God, a form of blessing on the Prophet, and some passages of the Ḳur-án respecting marriage. They all recite the Fátiḥah (or opening chapter of the Ḳur-án), after which the bridegroom pays the money. The latter and the bride's deputy then seat themselves on the ground, face to face, and grasp each other's right hand, raising the thumbs, and pressing them against each other. Previously to the khuṭbeh, the person who recites this formula places a handkerchief over the two joined hands; and after the khuṭbeh he dictates to the two contracting parties what they are to say. The betrother generally uses the following or a similar form of words: "I betroth to thee my daughter [or her for whom I act as deputy] such a one [naming the bride], the virgin [or the adult virgin, etc.], for a dowry of such an amount." The bridegroom answers, "I accept from thee her betrothal to myself." This is all that is absolutely necessary; but the address and reply are usually repeated a second and third time, and are often expressed in fuller forms of words. The contract is concluded with the recital of the Fátiḥah by all persons present.

This betrothal, or marriage-contract, is often performed several years before the wedding, when the two parties are yet children, or during the infancy of the girl; but most commonly not more than about eight or ten days before that event. The household furniture and dress prepared for the bride are sent by her family to the bridegroom's house, usually conveyed by a train of camels, two or three or more days before she is conducted thither.

The feasts and processions which are now to be mentioned are only observed in the case of a virgin-bride; a widow or divorced woman being remarried in a private manner. I describe them chiefly in accordance with the usages of Cairo, which appear to me most agreeable, in general, with the descriptions and allusions in the "Thousand and One Nights." The period most commonly approved for the wedding is the eve of Friday, or that of Monday. Previously to this event, the bridegroom once or twice or more frequently gives a feast to his friends; and for several nights, his house and the houses of his near neighbours are usually illuminated by numerous clusters of lamps, or by lanterns, suspended in front of them; some, to cords drawn across the street. To these or other cords are also suspended small flags, or square pieces of silk, each of two different colours, generally red and green. Some say that the feast or feasts should be given on the occasion of the marriage-contract; others, on the actual wedding; others, again, on both these occasions.[1]

The usual custom of the people of Cairo is to give a feast on the night before the nuptials, and another on the wedding night; but some begin their feasts earlier. Respecting marriage-feasts, the Prophet said,

[1] Nuzhet el-Mutaämmil, section 8.

"The first day's feast is an incumbent duty; and the second day's, a sunneh ordinance; and the third day's, for ostentation and notoriety:" and he forbade eating at the feast of the ostentatious.[1] It is a positive duty to accept an invitation to a marriage-feast or other lawful entertainment; but the guest is not obliged to eat.[2] The persons invited and all intimate friends generally send presents of provisions of some kind a day or two before. The Prophet taught that marriage-feasts should be frugal: the best that *he* gave was with one goat.[3] He approved of demonstrations of joy at the celebration of a marriage with songs, and according to one tradition by the beating of deffs (or tambourines); but in another tradition the latter practice is condemned.[4] The preferable mode of entertaining the guests is by the performance of a zikr.

On the day preceding that on which she is conducted to the bridegroom's house, the bride goes to the public bath, accompanied by a number of her female relations and friends. The procession generally pursues a circuitous route, for the sake of greater display; and on leaving the house, turns to the right. In Cairo, the bride walks under a canopy of silk borne by four men, with one of her near female

[1] Nuzhet el-Mutaämmil, section 8.
[2] Ibid.; and Mishkát el-Maṣábeeḥ, ii. 105.
[3] Mishkát el-Maṣábeeḥ, ii. 104.
[4] Nuzhet el-Mutaämmil, loco laudato; and Mishkát el-Maṣábeeḥ, ii. 89.

relations on each side of her. Young unmarried girls walk before her; these are preceded by the married ladies; and the procession is headed and closed by a few musicians with drums and hautboys. The bride wears a kind of pasteboard crown or cap, and is completely veiled from the view of spectators by a Kashmeer shawl placed over her crown and whole person; but some handsome ornaments of the head are attached externally. The other women are dressed in the best of their walking-attire. In the case, however, of a bride of high rank, or of wealth, and often in the case of one belonging to a family of the middle class, the ladies ride upon high-saddled asses, without music or canopy; and the bride is only distinguished by a Kashmeer shawl instead of the usual black silk covering, one or more eunuchs sometimes riding at the head. In the bath, after the ordinary operations of washing, etc., a feast is made, and the party are often entertained by female singers.

Having returned in the same manner to her home, the bride's friends there partake of a similar entertainment with her. Her hands and feet are then stained with hennà, and her eyes ornamented with koḥl; and her friends give her small presents of money, and take their leave. "It is a sunneh ordinance that the bride wash her feet in a clean vessel, and sprinkle the water in the corners of the chamber, that a blessing may result from this. She should also brighten her face, and put on the best of her apparel, and adorn her eyes with koḥl, and stain [her hands and feet] with ḥennà [as above mentioned]; and she should abstain, during the first week, from eating anything that contains mustard, and from vinegar, and sour apples."[1]

The bride is conducted to the house of the bridegroom (on the following day) in the same manner as to the bath, or with more pomp. In Cairo, the bridal processions of persons of very high rank are conducted with singular display. The train is usually headed by buffoons and musicians, and a water-carrier loaded with a goat's-skin filled with sand and water, of very great weight, which is often borne for many hours before (as well as during) the procession, merely to amuse the spectators by this feat of strength. Then follow (interrupted by groups of male or female dancers, jugglers, and the like) numerous decorated open waggons or cars, each of which contains several members of some particular trade or art engaged in their ordinary occupations, or one such person with attendants: in one, for instance, a kahwejee, with his assistants and pots and cups and fire, making coffee for the spectators: in a second, makers of sweetmeats: in a third, makers of pancakes (faṭeerehs): in a fourth, silk-lace manufacturers: in a fifth, a silk-weaver, with his loom: in a sixth, tinners of copper vessels, at their

[1] Nuzhet el-Mutaämmil, l.l.; Mishkát el-Maṣábeeḥ, ii. 89.

work: in a seventh, white-washers, whitening over and over again a wall: in short, almost every manufacture and trade has its representatives in a separate waggon. El-Jabartee describes a procession of this kind in which there were upwards of seventy parties of different trades and arts, each party in a separate waggon, besides buffoons, wrestlers, dancers, and others; followed by various officers, the eunuchs of the bride's family, ladies of the ḥareem with their attendants, then the bride in a European carriage, a troop of memlooks clad in armour, and a Turkish band of music. It was a procession of which the like had not before been seen.[1]

The bride and her party, having arrived at the house, sit down to a repast. The bridegroom does not yet see her. He has already been to the bath, and at nightfall he goes in procession with a number of his friends to a mosque, to perform the night-prayers. He is accompanied by musicians and singers, or by chanters of lyric odes in praise of the Prophet, and by men bearing cressets—poles with cylindrical frames of iron at the top filled with flaming wood; and on his return, most of his other attendants bear lighted wax candles and bunches of flowers.

Returned to his house, he leaves his friends in a lower apartment, and goes up to the bride, whom he

[1] Account of the Emeer Moḥammad Agha El-Bároodee, obituary, year 1205.

finds seated, with a shawl thrown over her head, so as to conceal her face completely, and attended by one or two females. The latter he induces to retire by means of a small present. He then gives a present of money to the bride, as "the price of uncovering the face," and having removed the covering (saying as he does so, "In the name of God, the Compassionate, the Merciful"), he beholds her, generally for the first time. On the occasion of this first visit, which is called the "dukhool" or "dukhleh," he is recommended "to perfume himself, and to sprinkle some sugar and almonds on the head of the bride and on that of each woman with her (this practice being established by existing usage and by traditions): also, when he approaches her, he should perform the prayers of two rek'ahs, and she should do the same if able: then he should take hold of the hair over her forehead, and say, 'O God, bless me in my wife, and bless my wife in me! O God, bestow upon me [offspring] by her, and bestow upon her [offspring] by me! O God, unite us, as thou hast united, happily; and separate us, when thou separatest, happily!'"[1]

An astrological calculation is often made with the view of determining by what sign of the zodiac the two persons are influenced who contemplate becoming man and wife, and thence ascertaining whether they will agree. This is often done in the present day by

[1] Nuzhet el-Mutaämmil, section 8.

adding together the numerical values of the letters composing his or her name and that of the mother, and, if I remember right, subtracting from 12 the whole sum if this is less than 12, or what remains after subtracting, or dividing, by 12. Thus is obtained the number of the sign. The twelve signs, commencing with Aries, correspond respectively with the elements of fire, earth, air, water, fire, earth, and so on; and if the signs of the two parties indicate the same element, it is inferred that they will agree; but if they indicate different elements, the inference is that the one will be affected by the other in the same manner as the element of the one is by that of the other: thus, if the element of the man is fire, and that of the woman, water, he will be subject to her rule. Among other calculations of the same kind is the following:—The numerical values of the letters composing the name of each of the two parties are added together, and one of these two sums is subtracted from the other: if the remainder is an uneven number, the inference is unfavourable; but if even, the reverse.

Next to the service of the husband or master, the care of her children, and attending to other indispensable domestic duties, the most important occupation of the wife is that of spinning or weaving or needle-work. "Sitting for an hour employed with the distaff is better for women," said the Prophet, "than a year's worship; and for every piece of cloth woven of the thread spun by them they shall receive the reward of a martyr." — 'Áisheh, the Prophet's wife, thus declared the merit of spinning:—"Tell the women what I say: There is no woman who spins until she hath clothed herself but all the angels in the Seven Heavens pray for forgiveness of her sins; and she will go forth from her grave on the day of judgment wearing a robe of Paradise and with a veil upon her head, and before her shall be an angel and on her right an angel who will hand her a draught of the water of Selsebeel, the fountain of Paradise; and another angel will come to her, and carry her upon his wings, and bear her to Paradise. And when she enters Paradise, eighty thousand maidens will meet her, each maiden bringing a different robe; and she will have mansions of emeralds with three hundred doors, at each of which will stand an angel with a present from the Lord of the Throne."[1]—The arts above mentioned are pursued by the females in the ḥareems of the middle and higher classes. Their leisure-hours are mostly spent in working with the needle; particularly in embroidering handkerchiefs, head-veils, etc., upon a frame called mensej, with coloured silks and gold. Many women, even in the houses of the wealthy, replenish their private purses by ornamenting handkerchiefs and other things in this manner, and employing a delláleh (or female broker)

[1] Nuzhet el-Mutaämmil, section 7.

to take them to the market, or to other ḥareems, for sale.[1]

The separation of the sexes undoubtedly promotes the free intercourse of people of the same sex and of different ranks, who thus are able to associate together, regardless of difference of wealth or station, without the risk of occasioning unequal matrimonial connections. This separation is therefore felt by neither sex as oppressive, but is regarded by them as productive of results which constitute the Muslim's chief enjoyments,—the highest degree of domestic comfort, and the most free and extensive society of his fellow men. Thus it is with both sexes; and neither would give up the pleasure that they hence derive for a different system of society, somewhat extending their domestic intercourse, but often destroying the pleasures of home, and contracting into a compass comparatively narrow the fellowship which they enjoyed abroad.

I must now remark upon some other effects of the same system. First, the restriction of intercourse between the sexes before marriage renders indispensable, to some, the facility of divorce; for it would be unjust for a man who finds himself disappointed in his expectations of a wife, whom he has never before seen, not to be enabled to put her away. Secondly, it sometimes renders indispensable the licence of polygamy; for a man who finds his first wife unsuited to him may

[1] Modern Egyptians, ch. vi.

not be able to divorce her without reducing her to want; and the licence of polygamy becomes as necessary in this case as that of divorce in another. Thirdly, the liberty of polygamy renders the facility of divorce more desirable for the happiness of women; since, when a man has two or more wives, and one of them is dissatisfied with her situation, he is enabled to liberate her. Fourthly, the licence of divorce often acts as a check upon that of polygamy; for the fear of being obliged, by the influence of his first wife, or by that of her relations, to divorce her if he take a second, often prevents a man from doing this. Thus both these licences are required by the most important principle of the constitution of Muslim society, and each is productive of some moral benefit. In considering the question of their expediency, we should also remember that barrenness is much more common in hot climates than in those which are temperate.

The Christian scheme is plainly opposed to polygamy; but as to divorce, some have contended that it only forbids putting away a wife against her will, unless for one cause.[1] Christians are often most unjust in their condemnation of Muslim laws and tenets, and especially condemn those which agree with the Mosaic code and the practices of holy men; such as polygamy (which Moḥammad *limited*), divorce, war for the

[1] "The Protestants of Hungary admit the plea of 'irrevocabile odium.'"—Urquhart's Spirit of the East, ii. 416.

defence of religion, purifications, and even minor matters.[1] Moḥammad endeavoured to remove one of the chief causes of polygamy and divorce, by recommending that a man should see a woman whom he proposed to take as his wife.[2] We might imagine that he could have made these practices less common than they now are, and always have been, among his followers, had he given more licence, allowing the man to enjoy a limited association with the object of his choice in the presence of her female or male relations (the former of whom might be veiled), without infringing further the general law of the separation of the sexes. But he saw that such liberty would very seldom, if ever, be allowed: scarcely any parents among the Arabs, except those of the lower classes, permit the little licence which he recommended. Instead of condemning him for allowing a plurality of wives, I think we should be more reasonable if we commended him for diminishing and restricting the number. I think, too, that as Moses allowed his people for the hardness of their hearts to put away their wives,

[1] A religious lady once asked me if I so conformed with the manners of the Easterns as to eat in their "beastly manner." I replied, "Do not call it a 'beastly manner:' call it the manner of our Lord and his Apostles." But some excuse may be made in this case. I was determined, when I first went to the East, never to conform to the practice of eating with the fingers when I could avoid it; however, after I had first seen the manner of doing this, I immediately adopted the custom, and continued it.

[2] Mishkát el-Maṣábeeḥ, ii. 81.

and God denounced not polygamy when the patriarchs practised it, we should be more consistent as believers in the Scriptures if we admitted the permission of these practices to be more conducive to morality than their prohibition, among a people similar to the ancient Jews to whom Moses allowed such liberty. As to the privilege which Moḥammad assumed to himself, of having a greater number of wives than he allowed to others, I have elsewhere remarked,[1] that, in doing so, he may have been actuated by the want of male offspring as much as impelled by voluptuousness.

"On the subject of polygamy," says a writer who has deeply studied Muslim institutions and their effects, "a European has all the advantage in discussion with a Turkish woman, because her feelings are decidedly on the side of her antagonists; but then she has a tremendous power of reply, in the comparison of the practical effects of the two systems, and in the widely spread rumours of the heartlessness and the profligacy of Europe. All the convictions of our habits and laws stand in hostile array against the country where the principle of polygamy is admitted into the laws of the state; but yet, while we reproach Islamism with polygamy, Islamism may reproach us with practical polygamy, which, unsanctioned by law

[1] Selections from the Ḳur-án, 1st. ed., p. 59.

and reproved by custom, adds degradation of the mind to dissoluteness of morals."[1]

It should further be remarked that by sanctioning polygamy Moḥammad did not make the practice general: nay, he could not. It is a licence for the hard-hearted, which restrains them from worse conduct, and in some cases, as already shown, a resource for the tender-hearted. "The permission," observes the author just cited, "does not alter the proportions of men and women. While, therefore, the law of nature renders this practice an impossibility as regards the community, it is here still further restrained among the few who have the means of indulging in it, both by the domestic unquiet that results from it, and by the public censure and reprobation of which it is the object."

I have remarked in a former work that polygamy "is more rare among the higher and middle classes [in Egypt, and I believe in other Arab countries] than it is among the lower orders; and it is not very common among the latter. A poor man may indulge himself with two or more wives, each of whom may be able, by some art or occupation, nearly to provide her own subsistence; but most persons of the higher and middle orders are deterred from doing so by the

[1] Urquhart's Spirit of the East, ii. 415–416. See the two chapters on "the life of the Harem" and "State of Women," which I think the most valuable portion of the book.

consideration of the expense and discomfort which they would incur. A man having a wife who has the misfortune to be barren, and being too much attached to her to divorce her, is sometimes induced to take a second wife, merely in the hope of obtaining offspring; and from the same motive he may take a third, and a fourth; but fickle passion is the most evident and common motive both to polygamy and to repeated divorces. They are comparatively few who gratify this passion by the former practice. I believe that not more than one husband among twenty has two wives."[1]

I hope I have shown that though I consider polygamy as necessary in the constitution of Muslim society, to prevent a profligacy that would be worse than that which prevails to so great a degree in European countries, where people are united in marriage after an intimate mutual acquaintance, I consider it as a necessary *evil.* When two or more wives of the same man live together, or when they visit each other, feelings of jealousy are generally felt and often manifested, and especially on the part of the wife or wives who cannot claim precedence by having been married before the other or others, or by reason of being more favoured by the husband.[2] The wife first

[1] Modern Egyptians, ch. vi.

[2] A fellow-wife is called, in Arabic, "ḍarrah," a word derived from "ḍarar," which signifies "injury," because fellow-wives usually

married usually enjoys the highest rank: therefore parents often object to giving a daughter in marriage to a man who has already another wife; and it frequently happens that the woman who is sought in marriage objects to such a union. The law provides in some measure against the discomforts arising from polygamy, by giving to each wife a claim to a distinct lodging, affording conveniences for sleeping, cooking, etc.; and further enjoins the husband to be strictly impartial to his wives in every respect. But fruitfulness and superior beauty are qualifications that often enable a second, third, or fourth wife to usurp the place of the first; though in many cases, as I have already remarked, the lasting favourite is not the most handsome.

There are, however, many instances of sincere affection existing in the hearts of fellow-wives. The following story of two wives of the father of El-Jabartee, the modern Egyptian historian, related by himself, and of undoubted truth, is a pleasing example.—Speaking of the first of these two wives, the historian says,—

"Among her acts of conjugal piety and submission was this, that she used to buy for her husband beautiful

experience injurious treatment, one from another. The word "ḍarrah," in vulgar or colloquial Arabic (by substituting a soft for an emphatic *d*, and *u* for *a*), is pronounced "durrah," which properly signifies "a parrot." "The life of a fellow-wife is bitter" ("'eeshet ed-durrah murrah") is a common proverb. [Eṭ-Ṭantáwee.]

slave girls, with her own wealth, and deck them with ornaments and apparel, and so present them to him, confidently looking to the reward and recompense which she should receive [in Paradise] for such conduct. He took, in addition to her, many other wives from among free women, and bought female slaves; but she did not in consequence conceive any of that jealousy which commonly affects women. Among other strange events which happened was the following. When the subject of this memoir [the author's father] performed the pilgrimage in the year 1156 [A.D. 1743–44], he became acquainted at Mekkeh with the sheykh 'Omar El-Ḥalabee who commissioned him to purchase for him a white female slave, having such and such qualifications. So when he returned from the pilgrimage, he searched for female slaves among the slave-dealers, to choose from them such a one as was wanted, and ceased not until he found the object of his desire, and bought her. He brought her to his wife, to remain with her until he should send her with a person to whom he was commissioned to entrust her for the journey; and when the period at which she was to depart arrived, he informed his wife of it, that she might prepare the provisions for the way, and other necessaries. But she said to him, 'I have conceived a great love for this maid, and I cannot endure separation from her: I have no children, and I have taken her as a daughter.' The girl Zeleekha also wept, and said, 'I will not part from my mistress, nor ever leave her.' 'Then what is to be done?' he asked. She answered, 'I will pay her price from my own property, and do thou buy another.' He did so. She then emancipated the girl, gave her to him by a marriage-contract, prepared her paraphernalia, and furnished for her a separate apartment; and he took her as his wife in the year 1165. The former wife could not bear to be separated from her even for an hour, although she had become her fellow-wife, and borne him children. In the year 1182, the [emancipated] slave fell sick, and she [the first wife] fell sick on account of her [friend's] sickness. The illness increased upon both of them; and in the morning the slave arose, and looked at her mistress when she seemed about to die, and wept, and said, 'O my God and my Lord, if Thou hast decreed the death of my mistress, make my day to be before her day.' Then she lay down, and her disease increased, and she died the next night; and they wrapped her up by the side of her mistress. And her mistress awoke at the close of the night, and felt her with her hand, and began to say, 'Zeleekha! Zeleekha!' They said to her, 'She is asleep.' But she replied, 'My heart telleth me that she is dead: and I saw in my sleep what indicated this event.' They then said to her, 'May thy life be prolonged!'[1] And when she had

[1] This is the usual way of informing a person that another is

thus ascertained the event, she raised herself, and sat up, and said, 'No life remaineth to me after her.' And she wept and wailed until the day appeared, when they began to prepare for the speedy burial of the slave; and they washed the corpse before her, and carried it to the grave. Then she returned to her bed, and fell into the agonies of death, and died at the close of the day; and on the following day they carried her corpse to the grave in like manner."[1]

dead. Many say in the same case, "Mayest thou live!" and then being asked, "Who is dead?" mention the name.

[1] El-Jabartee's History, vol. i., obituary of the year 1188.

CHAPTER X.

SLAVERY.

A SLAVE, among Muslims, is either a person taken captive in war, or carried off by force, and being at the time of capture an infidel; or the offspring of a female slave by another slave or by any man who is not her owner, or by her owner if he does not acknowledge himself to be the father: but the offspring of a male slave by a free woman is free. A person who embraces the Mohammadan faith after having been made a slave does not by this act become free, unless he flies from a foreign infidel master to a Muslim country and there becomes a Mohammadan. A person cannot have as a slave one whom he acknowledges to be within the prohibited degrees of marriage. The slaves of the Arabs are mostly from Abyssinia and the Negro countries: a few, in the houses of very wealthy individuals, are from Georgia and Circassia.

Slaves have no civil liberty, but are entirely under the authority of their owners, whatever may be the religion, sex, or age, of the latter; and can possess no property, unless by the owner's permission. The owner is entire master, while he pleases, of the person and goods of his slave, and of the offspring of his female slave, which, if his, or presumed to be his, he may recognize as his own legitimate child, or not: the child, if recognized by him, enjoys the same privileges as the offspring of a free wife; and if not recognized by him, is his slave. The master may even kill his own slave with impunity for any offence; and he incurs but a slight punishment (as imprisonment for a period at the discretion of the judge) if he kills him wantonly. He may give away or sell his slaves, excepting in some cases which will be mentioned; and may marry them to whom he will, but not separate them when married. A slave, however, according to most of the doctors, cannot have more than two wives at the same time.

Unemancipated slaves, at the death of their master, become the property of his heirs; and when an emancipated slave dies, leaving no male descendants or collateral relations, the master is the heir; or, if the master be dead, his heirs inherit the slave's property. As a slave enjoys less advantages than a free person, the law in some cases ordains that his punishment for an offence shall be half of that to which the free is liable for the same offence, or even less than half: if it be a fine or pecuniary compensation, it must be paid by the owner to the amount, if necessary, of the value of the slave, or the slave must be given in compensation.

When a man, from being the husband, becomes the master, of a slave, the marriage is dissolved, and he cannot continue to live with her but as her master, enjoying, however, all a master's privileges, unless he emancipates her, in which case he may again take her as his wife with her consent. In like manner, when a woman, from being the wife, becomes the possessor, of a slave, the marriage is dissolved, and cannot be renewed unless she emancipates him, and he consents to the re-union.

Complete and immediate emancipation is sometimes granted to a slave gratuitously, or for a future pecuniary compensation. It is conferred by means of a written document, or by a verbal declaration (expressed in the words, "Thou art free," or some similar phrase) in the presence of two witnesses, or by returning the certificate of sale obtained from the former owner. Future emancipation is sometimes covenanted to be granted on the fulfilment of certain conditions, and more frequently to be conferred on the occasion of the owner's death. In the latter case the owner cannot sell the slave to whom he has made this promise: and, as he cannot alienate by will more than one-third of the whole property that he leaves, the law ordains that if the value of the said slave exceeds that portion, the slave must obtain and pay the additional sum.

When a female slave has borne a child to her master, and he acknowledges the child to be his own, he cannot sell this slave, and she becomes free on his death.

Abyssinian and white female slaves are kept by many men of the middle and higher classes, and often instead of wives, as requiring less expense and being more subservient; but they are generally indulged with the same luxuries as free ladies, their vanity is gratified by costly dresses and ornaments, and they rank high above free servants; as do also the male slaves. Those called Abyssinians appear to be a mixed race between negroes and whites, and are from the territories of the Gallas. They are mostly kidnapped and sold by their own countrymen. The negro female slaves, as few of them have considerable personal attractions (which is not the case with the Abyssinians, many of whom are very beautiful), are usually employed only in cooking and other menial offices. The female slaves of the higher classes are often instructed in plain needlework and embroidery, and sometimes in music and dancing. Formerly many of them possessed sufficient literary accomplishments to quote largely from esteemed poems, or even to compose extemporary verses, which they would often accompany with the lute.

Slaves of either sex are generally treated with kindness; but at first they are usually importuned, and not unfrequently used with much harshness, to induce them to embrace the Mohammadan faith;

which almost all of them do. Their services are commonly light: the usual office of the male white slave, who is called "memlook," is that of a page or a military guard. Eunuchs are employed as guardians of the women, but only in the houses of men of high rank or great wealth. On account of the important and confidential office which they fill, they are generally treated in public with especial consideration. I used to remark, in Cairo, that few persons saluted me with a more dignified and consequential air than these pitiable but self-conceited beings. Most of them are Abyssinians or Negroes. Indeed, the slaves in general take too much advantage of the countenance of their masters, especially when they belong to men in power. The master is bound to afford his slaves proper food and clothing, or to let them work for their own support, or to sell, give away, or liberate them. It is, however, considered disgraceful for him to sell a slave who has been long in his possession; and it seldom happens that a master emancipates a female slave without marrying her to some man able to support her, or otherwise providing for her.

The Prophet strongly enjoined the duty of kindness to slaves. "Feed your memlooks," said he, "with food of that which ye eat, and clothe them with such clothing as ye wear; and command them not to do that for which they are unable."[1] These precepts are

[1] Nuzhet el-Mutaämmil, section 9.

generally attended to, either entirely or in a great degree. Some other sayings of the Prophet on this subject well deserve to be mentioned—as the following:—"He who beats his slave without fault, or slaps him on the face, his atonement for this is freeing him." —"A man who behaves ill to his slave will not enter into Paradise."—"Whoever is the cause of separation between mother and child, by selling or giving, God will separate him from his friends on the day of resurrection."—"When a slave wishes well to his master, and worships God well, for him are double rewards."[1]

It is related of 'Othmán, "that he twisted the ear of a memlook belonging to him, on account of disobedience, and afterwards, repenting of it, ordered him to twist *his* ear in like manner: but he would not. 'Othmán urged him, and the memlook advanced, and began to wring it by little and little. He said to him, 'Wring it hard; for I cannot endure the punishment of the day of judgment [on account of this act].' The memlook answered, 'O my master, the day that thou fearest, I also fear.'"—"It is related also of Zeyn el-'Ábideen, that he had a memlook who seized a sheep, and broke its leg; and he said to him, 'Why didst thou this?' He answered, 'To provoke thee to anger.' 'And I,' said he, 'will provoke to anger him who taught thee; and he is Iblees: go, and be free, for the sake of God.'"[2]—Many similiar anecdotes might be added;

[1] Mishkát el-Maṣábeeḥ, ii. 140, 141 [2] Nuzhet el-Mutaämmil, l.l.

but the general assertions of travellers in the East are more satisfactory evidence in favour of the humane conduct of most Muslims to their slaves.

It sometimes happens, though rarely, that free girls are sold as slaves.[1] A remarkable instance is related in the Mir-át ez-Zemán.[2]—Fátimeh, surnamed Ghareeb, a slave of the Khaleefeh El-Moaṭaṣim, the son of Hároon, was a poetess, accomplished in singing and calligraphy, and extremely beautiful. Her mother was an orphan; and Jaafar, the famous Wezeer of Hároon Er-Rasheed, took her as his wife; but his father, Yaḥyà, reproached him for marrying a woman whose father and mother were unknown, and he therefore removed her from his own residence to a neighbouring house, where he frequently visited her; and she bore him a daughter, the above-mentioned Ghareeb, and died. Jaafar committed her infant to the care of a Christian woman to nurse; and, on the overthrow of his family, this woman sold her young charge as a slave. El-Emeen, the successor of Er-Rasheed, bought her of a man named Sumbul, but never paid her price; and when he was killed, she returned to her former master; but on the arrival of El-Ma-moon at Baghdád, she was described to him, and he compelled Sumbul to sell her to him. This Sumbul loved her so passionately that he died of grief at her loss.

[1] See Modern Egyptians, ch. vi.

[2] Events of the year 227.

On the death of El-Ma-moon, his successor, El-Moạtaṣim, bought her for a hundred thousand dirhems, and emancipated her. The historian adds that she composed several well-known airs and verses.

CHAPTER XI.

CEREMONIES OF DEATH.

THE ceremonies attendant upon death and burial are nearly the same in the cases of men and women. The face or the head of the dying person is turned towards the direction of Mekkeh. When the spirit is departing, the eyes are closed; and then, or immediately after, the women of the house commence a loud lamentation, in which many of the females of the neighbourhood generally come to join. Hired female mourners are also usually employed, each of whom accompanies her exclamations of "Alas for him!" etc. by beating a tambourine. If possible, the corpse is buried on the day of the death;[1] but when this cannot be done, the lamentation of the women is continued during the ensuing night; and a recitation of several chapters, or of the whole, of the Ḳur-án is performed by one or more men hired for the purpose.

[1] "When any one of you dies," said the Prophet, "you must not keep him in the house; but carry him quickly to his grave:" and again he said, "Be quick in lifting up a bier; for if the deceased be a good man, it is good to take him up quickly, and carry him to his grave. to cause the good to arrive at happiness; and if the deceased be a bad man, it is a wickedness which ye put from your neck." (Mishkát el-Maṣábeeḥ, i. 374, 387.)

The washing consists, first, in the performance of the ordinary ablution that is preparatory to prayer, with the exception of the cleansing of the mouth and nose, and secondly, in an ablution of the whole body with warm water and soap, or with water in which some leaves of the lote-tree have been boiled. The jaw is bound up, the eyes are closed, and the nostrils, etc., are stuffed with cotton; and the corpse is sprinkled with a mixture of water, pounded camphor, dried and pounded leaves of the lote-tree, and sometimes other dried and pulverized leaves, and with rose-water. The ankles are bound together;[1] and the hands placed upon the breast.

The grave-clothing of a poor man consists of a piece or two of cotton, or a kind of bag; but the corpse of a man of wealth is generally wrapped first in muslin, then in cotton cloth of a thicker texture, next in a piece of striped stuff of silk and cotton intermixed, or in a ḳafṭán (a long vest) of similar stuff merely stitched together, and over these is wrapped a Kashmeer shawl.[2] The colours most approved for

[1] Two customs, namely, tying the toes of the corpse, and placing a knife, or rather a sword, upon the body, are still common in some Muslim countries; but I did not hear of their being observed in Egypt, nor the custom of putting salt with the knife or sword. Iron and salt are both believed to repel genii, and to prevent their approach, and hence, perhaps, are thus used.

[2] It is a common custom for a Muslim, on a military expedition, or during a long journey, especially in the desert, to carry his grave-linen with him; for he is extremely careful that he may be buried according to the law.

the grave-clothes are white and green. The body thus shrouded is placed in a bier, which is usually covered with a Kashmeer shawl, and borne on the shoulders of three or four men, generally friends of the deceased.

There are some slight differences in the funeral ceremonies observed in different Arab countries; but a sufficient notion of them will be conveyed by briefly describing those which prevail in Cairo. The procession to the tomb is generally headed by a number of poor men, mostly blind, who, walking two and two, or three and three together, chant, in a melancholy tone, the profession (or two professions) of the faith, "There is no deity but God" and "Moḥammad is God's apostle," or sometimes other words. They are usually followed by some male relations and friends of the deceased; and these, by a group of schoolboys, chanting in a higher tone, and one of them bearing a copy of the Ḳur-án, or of one of its thirty sections, placed upon a kind of desk formed of palm-sticks, and covered with an embroidered kerchief. Then follows the bier, borne head-foremost. Friends of the deceased relieve one another in the office of carrying it; and casual passengers often take part in this service, which is esteemed highly meritorious. Behind the bier walk the female mourners, composing a numerous group, often more than a dozen; or, if of a wealthy family, they ride. Each of those who belong to the family of the deceased has a strip of cotton stuff or muslin, generally blue, bound round her head, over the head-veil, and carries a handkerchief, usually dyed blue (the colour of mourning), which she sometimes holds over her shoulders, and at other times twirls with both hands over her head or before her face, while she cries and shrieks almost incessantly; and the hired female mourners, accompanying the group, often celebrate the praises of the deceased, though this was forbidden by the Prophet. The funeral procession of a man of wealth is sometimes preceded by several camels, bearing bread and water to give to the poor at the tomb; and closed by the led horses of some of the attendants, and by a buffalo or other animal to be sacrificed at the tomb, where its flesh is distributed to the poor, to atone for some of the minor sins of the deceased.[1]

The bier used for conveying the corpse of a boy or a female has a cover of wood, over which a shawl is spread; and at the head is an upright piece of wood: upon the upper part of this, in the case of a boy, is fixed a turban, with several ornaments of female head-dress; and in the case of a female, it is similarly decked, but without the turban.

A short prayer is recited over the dead, either in a

[1] More than one is unusual; but at the funeral of Moḥammad 'Alee, which I witnessed in Cairo, about eighty buffaloes were thus driven in the procession.—E. S. P.

mosque or in a place particularly dedicated to this service in or adjacent to the burial-ground. The body is then conveyed, in the same manner as before, to the tomb. This is a hollow, oblong vault, one side of which faces the direction of Mekkeh, generally large enough to contain four or more bodies, and having an oblong monument of stone or brick constructed over it, with a stela at the head and foot. Upon the former of these two stelae (which is often inscribed with a text from the Ḳur-án, and the name of the deceased, with the date of his death), a turban, cap, or other head-dress, is sometimes carved, showing the rank or class of the person or persons buried beneath ; and in many cases, a cupola supported by four walls, or by columns, is constructed over the smaller monument. The body is laid on its right side, or inclined by means of a few crude bricks, so that the face is turned towards Mekkeh ; and a person is generally employed to dictate to the deceased the answers which he should give when he is examined by the two angels Munkar and Nekeer. If the funeral be that of a person of rank or wealth, the bread and water before mentioned are then distributed to the poor.[1]

Towards the eve of the first Friday after the funeral, and often early in the morning of the Thursday, the women of the family of the deceased repeat their wailing in the house accompanied by some of

[1] See further Modern Egyptians, ch. xxviii.

their female friends: male friends of the deceased also visit the house shortly before or after sunset; and three or four persons are hired to perform a recitation of the whole of the Ḳur-án. On the following morning, some or all of the members of the deceased's family, but chiefly the women, visit the tomb; they or their servants carrying palm-branches, and sometimes sweet basil, to lay upon it, and often the visitors take with them some kind of food, as bread, pancakes, sweet cakes of different kinds, or dates, to distribute to the poor on this occasion. They recite portions of the Ḳur-án or employ people to recite it, as has been already mentioned.[1] These ceremonies are repeated on the same days of the next two weeks; and again on the eve and morning of the Friday which completes, or next follows, the first period of forty days after the funeral; whence this Friday is called El-Arba'een, or Jum'at el-Arba'een.

It is believed that the soul remains with the body until the expiration of the first night after the burial, when it departs to the place appointed for the abode of good souls until the last day, or to the appointed prisons in which wicked souls await their final doom; but with respect to the state of souls in the interval between death and judgment, there are various opinions which Sale thus states.[2] As to the souls of the good, he says, "1. Some say they stay near the

[1] See above, 23 and 24. [2] Preliminary Discourse, section iv.

sepulchres; with liberty, however, of going wherever they please; which they confirm from Moḥammad's manner of saluting them at their graves, and his affirming that the dead heard those salutations as well as the living, though they could not answer. Whence perhaps proceeded the custom of visiting the tombs of relations, so common among the Mohammadans. 2. Others imagine they are with Adam, in the lowest heaven; and also support their opinion by the authority of their prophet, who gave out that in his return from the upper heavens in his pretended night-journey, he saw there the souls of those who were destined to paradise on the right hand of Adam, and those who were condemned to hell on his left. 3. Others fancy the souls of believers remain in the well Zemzem, and those of infidels in a certain well in the province of Haḍramót, called Barahoot:[1] but this opinion is branded as heretical [?]. 4. Others say they stay near the graves for seven days; but that whither they go afterwards is uncertain. 5. Others that they are all in the trumpet, whose sound is to raise the dead. And 6. Others that the souls of the good dwell in the forms of white birds, under the throne of God. As to the condition of the souls of the wicked, the more orthodox held that they are offered by the angels to heaven, from whence being

[1] So in the Ḳámoos, and in my MS. of the 'Ajáïb el-Makhlooḳát of El-Ḳazweenee; but by Sale written "Borhût."

repulsed as stinking and filthy, they are offered to the earth; and, being also refused a place there, are carried down to the seventh earth, and thrown into a dungeon, which they call Sijjeen, under a green rock, or according to a tradition of Moḥammad, under the devil's jaw, to be there tormented till they are called up to be joined again to their bodies." But the souls of prophets are believed to be admitted immediately into paradise, and those of martyrs are said to rest in the crops of green birds which eat of the fruits of paradise and drink of its rivers.[1]

Of the opinions above mentioned, with respect to the souls of the faithful, I believe the first to be that which is most prevalent. It is generally said that these souls visit their respective graves every Friday; and according to some they return to their bodies on Friday, after the period of the afternoon prayers, and on Saturday and Monday; or on Thursday, Friday, and Saturday; and remain until sunrise.[2]—I believe also, from having heard frequent allusions made to it

[1] The Mohammadan law distinguishes several different descriptions of martyrs. This honourable title is given to the soldier who dies in fighting for the faith, or on his way to do so, or who dies almost immediately after his having been wounded when so engaged; to a person who innocently meets with his death from the hand of another; to a victim of the plague, who does not flee from the disease, or of dysentery; to a person who is drowned, and to one who is killed by the falling of a wall or any building.

[2] Murshid ez-Zoowár ilà Ḳuboor el-Abrár (the Director of the Visitors to the Tombs of the Just) by 'Abd-er-Raḥmán El-Khazrejee El-Anṣáree: MS. in my possession.

as a thing not to be doubted, that the opinion respecting the Well of Barahoot commonly prevails in the present day. El-Ḳazweenee says of it, "It is a well *near* Haḍramót; and the Prophet (God bless and save him!) said, 'In it are the souls of the infidels and hypocrites.' It is an 'Adite well [*i.e.* ancient, as though made by the old tribe of 'Ad], in a dry desert, and a gloomy valley; and it is related of 'Alee (may God be well pleased with him!), that he said, 'The most hateful of districts unto God (whose name be exalted!) is the Valley of Barahoot, in which is a well whose water is black and fetid, where the souls of the infidels make their abode.' El-Asma'ee hath related of a man of Haḍramót that he said, 'We find near Barahoot an extremely disgusting and fetid smell, and then news is brought to us of the death of a great man of the chiefs of the infidels.' It is related, also, that a man who passed a night in the Valley of Barahoot, said, 'I heard all the night [exclamations] of O Roomeh! O Roomeh! and I mentioned this to a learned man, and he told me that it was the name of the angel commissioned to keep guard over the souls of the infidels.'"[1]

[1] 'Ajáïb el-Makhlooḳát.

INDEX.

AUTHORS AND WORKS QUOTED.

(Authors' names are in small capitals; titles of books in italics. The figures refer to the pages of the present work.)

ERRATUM.

Page 44, note 1, *for* "fifteenth" *read* "fourteenth."